ART and MAN

BOOK THREE
THE MODERN WORLD

PETER H. BRIEGER

G. STEPHEN VICKERS

FREDERICK E. WINTER

CONSULTANTS:

William Withrow

K. English

A. Louise Griffith

HOLT, RINEHART AND WINSTON OF CANADA, LIMITED, TORONTO

ART AND MAN, BOOK III, is the third of a series of three books on the history of art published by Holt, Rinehart and Winston of Canada Limited.

AUTHORS

PETER H. BRIEGER, PH.D., F.S.A., (Head of the Department of Fine Art, University of Toronto)

G. STEPHEN VICKERS, M.A., (Professor, Department of Fine Art, University of Toronto)

FREDERICK E. WINTER, PH.D., (Associate Professor, Department of Fine Art, University of Toronto)

CONSULTANTS

WILLIAM WITHROW, B.A., (Director, The Art Gallery of Toronto)

K. ENGLISH, B.A., (Head of the Art Department, Earl Haig Secondary School, Willowdale)

A. LOUISE GRIFFITH, M.A., (Head of the English Department, Midland Avenue Collegiate Institute, Scarborough)

ISBN 0-03-926550-1

Copyright © 1964 by

HOLT, RINEHART AND WINSTON OF CANADA, LIMITED

Printed in Canada

4 5 - 71 70

Contents

Introduction

Modern art was born of a revolt against the art of the eighteenth century. In the confusion following the revolt, first one and then another part of Europe's heritage has been put to use by artists who, since the mid-nineteenth century, have gone outside the European tradition to borrow from the arts of the Orient, and of the primitive peoples. Only within the past fifty years has modern art become self-sustaining and able to grow within its own tradition.

Viewed in the perspective of a century, the nineteenth seems to show sharp stages of development about a generation apart, tending in one general direction. After 1890 the pattern is not as discernible. The revolutionary change at that time has been followed by artistic activities not easily reducible to any pattern. Much of the difficulty may be caused by sheer proximity: we may be sure that the present is more complex than will be the history of it. A history of modern art becomes, then, in its final stages a series of observations without much purposeful relation between them.

Leadership in the development of modern art was limited at the outset of this period to France and England, and during the middle years of the nineteenth century to France alone; but in the last quarter of the century, artists from all parts of Europe and even America began to play significant roles. Paris retained its position as the great clearing house of new artistic expressions until the Second World War. Today modern art has become modern *world* art, with many important centres of activity; and its practitioners are citizens of the world.

In the face of this last fact local activities circumscribed by national boundaries have rapidly lost what separate identity they once had. The easy circulation of artists and works of art have obliterated most frontiers. Nevertheless the history of the transmission, preservation and modification of forms derived from Europe is of special concern to North Americans.

There had long been lesser artistic provinces of European art within that continent—the Scandinavian countries, for instance—which had taken their direction from main European centres. The development of colonies extended provincialism to the American continents; but it was only one colonial culture, the United States, that outgrew this status to take a place as a major force in the twentieth century. Canadians can examine with profit what happened in the culture physically closest to her, if only to conclude that so-called "national" characteristics of both of American and Canadian art are in fact shared by both, and generally derive from common European sources.

The place of Canadian art in a history of modern art is necessarily more limited than it would be in a programme of studies centred solely on a national Canadian theme. But it is the art closest to us and, as such, demands attention. It colours our environment and should be our responsibility to know. Examined in its relation to modern art generally it can help fill in our understanding of our own country's cultural relations to the rest of the world. One of the dilemmas of isolation is reflected in the withering of French-Canadian artistic tradition which could not sustain itself. The history of the Group of Seven is an example of the intense but short-lived nationalism that was unable to support itself before the universal world of art of the post World War II period.

The chapters on Oriental and Primitive art in this book were not included simply because European artists began to take an interest in the creations of these alien cultures in the later 19th and 20th centuries: their interest at that time was vital but relatively short-lived. The arts of these now virtually dead cultures continue to provide a treasury of new experience to those artists and viewers who were born in the western tradition, and are therefore represented here although in a necessarily abbreviated outline. The great differences which separate the western tradition from either of the other two, provides just that opportunity for a comparison that effectively dissipates any notion that our own heritage is the only one possible. The study of western man's art has been the subject of three years' attention. It is fitting that by a comparison with the primitive world and with the oriental we see where western man started his course and in what direction he has gone.

G. S. V.
F. E. W.
P. H. B.

Fig. 1: LIBRARY—HOUSES OF PARLIAMENT, *Ottawa. T. Fuller. Begun 1859. (Courtesy, The Department of Fine Art, University of Toronto).*

Chapter I

MODERN ARCHITECTURE: THE NINETEENTH CENTURY

The evidence for the architectural history of the past 150 years is to be found in the appearance of the cities that grew mightily with the Industrial Revolution and the accompanying explosion of population. The centre of every city is crowded with commercial and public buildings, each of which varies widely in appearance from the other. The city's suburbs spread out to add the monotony of distance to the confusion of difference. The period shows nothing comparable to the orderly urban growth of eighteenth-century Bath (see Book I, page 176).

Even before the middle of the eighteenth century, we observe the first traces of appeal to historic styles for guidance. What was at the outset not much different from the revival of antiquity at the time of the Italian Renaissance became, by the nineteenth century, an effort to find in history complete equivalents for most contemporary needs. New kinds of buildings were coming into existence, materials and techniques were changing as well, but the final design went back to a time before these changes had begun.

The last renewal of interest in Classic architecture began shortly before 1750. It reached its climax in the years of the French Revolution and the Napoleonic empire, and by 1850 had ceased to be a force. To distinguish this revival from earlier revivals, it is generally called Neoclassicism. Begun as a revolt against the trivialities of the Rococo, it paralleled in art the attacks

1

Fig. 3: BRANDENBURG GATE, *Berlin. K. Langhans. 1788-91.*

by serious and reasonable men on the emptiness and corruption of the old aristocracy. The architectural forms, which recalled the political and moral grandeur of Athens and Rome, were simple and permanent in appearance compared to the fragile and intricate systems of the Rococo. Thus, the BRANDENBURG GATE, Berlin, (Fig. 3), begun in 1788 as a modified version of another gate, the Propylaea, Athens, sternly declared the stability of the Prussian state. The massive gate stood darkly silhouetted against the great avenue linking Potsdam, the place of the ruler's residence, with his capital, Berlin, and was the setting for royal entries into the latter city.

To cite another instance: in the United States, the first state Capitol built after the War of Independence, that at Richmond, Virginia, (Fig. 4) took the form of a Roman temple. A temple was hardly the proper building for a legislature unless republicanism was a religion; but the political faith of Thomas Jefferson, its designer, was precisely that. Nor was it easy to house a building of more than one storey in a temple. The difficulty was not insuperable, but for more than a century its very existence indicated the basic problem of the architect, namely, that of covering a structure built for one purpose with the dress of a building made for quite another.

At the time of the Renaissance, Italian architects had paid considerable attention to Roman buildings, but only in order to copy ornamental details or to derive certain rules of proportion, and exceptionally, to obtain an understanding that produced not imitations of the old but up-to-date equivalents of them. The new students of antiquity went much further, and in their books they gave a more nearly exact record of whole buildings. Rome continued to be a mine of information, but for the first time English and French architects went further afield to discover Greek architecture, a preference for which grew steadily during the Neo-classic phase. Greece was even more remote than Rome from the extravagances of Baroque and Rococo, and the Doric order especially seemed to represent a primeval simplicity to which the values of permanence, dignity, restraint, and clarity were easily attached. The Brandenburg Gate is an early instance of this admiration.

The books, recording these findings, were to be found as often in a gentleman's library as in an architect's office. The study of them simultaneously educated the client's taste and guided the designer's pencil. It will be noted that readers of the books were looking at engravings, not real buildings, and saw architecture as the surface skin, not as the whole structure.

Fig. 4: STATE CAPITOL, *Richmond, Virginia. Thomas Jefferson. Begun 1789—wings added later. (Courtesy, Virginia Chamber of Commerce).*

There was little church building during the latter eighteenth century, and still less during the troubled Napoleonic era. When a new religious fervour appeared at the end of the wars, it brought to the front another historic style, the Gothic. This second revival was as old as Neo-Classicism but had developed more slowly, chiefly among the English, many of whom looked upon mediaeval churches as Britain's true antiquity. At first, in a minority movement directly opposed to Neo-Classicism, the Gothicists advocated an art where personal fancy replaced the rules and systems of the Neo-Classicists. The great majority of the early buildings were designed by amateurs, usually literary people, and were limited to private houses.

The most famous is STRAWBERRY HILL, (Fig. 5), just outside London, the residence of Horace Walpole who, beginning about 1750,

worked on it for over twenty years. Walpole was the author of a mediaeval novel of knights and fair ladies: his house and his novel are equally remote from the Middle Ages. Only from a distance are the battlements and pointed windows Gothic; inside, the walls, ceilings, and mantelpieces are covered with papier-mâché adaptations of ornaments copied from mediaeval tombs in English churches. At this stage, Gothic was not architecture, but merely ornamental trim.

More fateful than this decorative overlay, since it spread beyond the Gothic Revival, was the rejection of symmetry of plan and elevation. Viewed from different points in the gardens, the mass of Strawberry Hill presented asymmetrical silhouettes, and the impressive, direct approach and elaborate entrances of earlier country houses, such as Blenheim, were gone

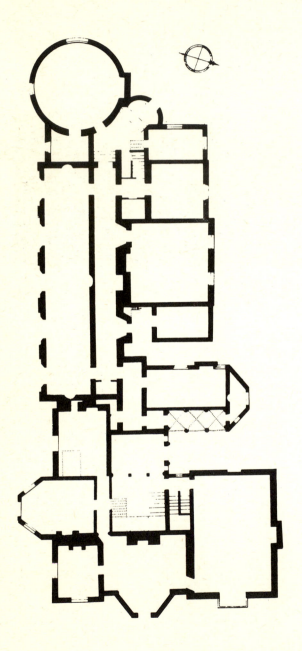

Plan, STRAWBERRY HILL, *1749-1781*.

The southern end was already built when Walpole purchased the house. Over a period of thirty years, he extended it north by stages. The portion of the building that shows to the left of the tower in Fig. 5 was added in the nineteenth century.

Fig. 5: STRAWBERRY HILL, *Twickenham near London, England. Horace Walpole and friends. 1749-1781—(Courtesy, Art Reference Bureau).*

(see Book II, Fig. 167). English parks, which had been an extension of the regularity of the house, were now laid out to suggest, to the stroller about the grounds, a natural setting into which the house fitted as in a series of pictures. From being a demonstration of man's mastery of his environment, parks had become the evidence of his eagerness to be absorbed in it.

Inside Strawberry Hill, there were rooms so different one from another in all their dimensions, decorations, and lighting that the wandering visitor was confronted with surprise after surprise; and if he was a rational man he must have wondered at the need for such a maze of rooms. Mediaeval domestic architecture also had no planned sequences of rooms or balanced symmetry because original unevenness of site, variations of use, and the additions demanded by an increasing household produced irregularities. The Gothic revivalist employed irregularities for artistic reasons only. This release from a fixed plan brought freedom to the designer, but it was more than a century before he gained the skill to combine informality of plan with convenience of use.

At the beginning of the nineteenth century, the popularity of mediaeval poetry and the vogue for the novels of Sir Walter Scott aroused a more general interest. The British Isles were soon sprinkled with sham castles, and the vogue spread to the continent. After 1815, religion also nourished the revival and became, in fact, its chief patron. The Middle Ages had been an age of faith, the great cathedrals their lasting monuments. There were no great cathedrals built in the nineteenth century: the change in the position of the church in society, and the great shift from hand craftsmanship to industrial manufacture saw to that. The best that resulted was the building of small churches, representing the pockets of faith in a world oriented to very unspiritual ends.

Fig. 6: Houses of Parliament, *Westminster. Sir Charles Barry. Begun 1835—*
(Courtesy, National Buildings Record).

Yet, out of this failure, came an awareness of the problem of art in an industrial society, and, for a century, the debate on this problem was lively and important for all of the arts. No other revival left more than a trace after the period of its greatest fashion had ended.

Beginning with the universities, the Gothic Revival also steadily invaded the field of educational buildings and then of town halls, both institutions of mediaeval origin. Finally, Gothic style was chosen for the Houses of Parliament, Westminster (Fig. 6).

The replacement of the ancient palace, destroyed by fire in 1834, had been the occasion of debate as to which of the available past styles should be used. The victory of Gothic was a tribute to the principle of historic connection with the institution housed in it. The very appearance of the building became a warranty of age and respectability and a reminder of past glory. In this case, the Late Gothic dress was supposed to recall the glorious years of Tudor reign.

The Houses of Parliament are a grid in plan; therefore, unmediaeval but well suited to the uses of the building. Regularity is concealed by a forest of towers of different shapes placed over positions of special importance. The largest imitates a church tower; another, resembling a mediaeval town belfry, houses the clock; and the small ones are like the towers found on Tudor palaces. Seen as it should be from a distance, the structure presents the appearance of a mediaeval town skyline. The towers and the walls between them are so fretted with buttresses, panellings and window openings, which catch the shadow and modify the misty light of London, that for all their size the Houses of Parliament lack a feeling of ordered mass. This, the one seat of government, not conforming to the preferred Neo-classic model of the time, sheltered the government most obscurely constructed. Having no written constitution, its real power was hidden behind a show of ancient trappings.

During the nineteenth century, there were almost as many other revivals as there were

Fig. 7: ROYAL PAVILION, *Brighton, England. John Nash. 1815-1818— (Courtesy, National Buildings Record).*

sources to be tapped, though most of them were of shorter duration than the Neo-classic or Gothic. Around 1800, the Italian Villa began to compete with the Gothic as an informal country-house style. It had the same picturesque grouping of towers and wings of different shapes but substituted round-headed, or lintelled, openings. In the 1830's, examples of High Renaissance Italian architecture, like the Farnese Palace, were considered the proper setting for the palatial grandeur of gentlemen's clubs in London, and for business blocks, the palaces of industry. About the same time, the Romanesque attracted those who wanted mediaeval associations without the suspicion of attachment to pre-Reformation religious beliefs. More exotic revivals still were the Egyptian, favoured for prisons and cemetery gates, and the Moorish, equally suitable for a pleasure house, the ROYAL PAVILION, BRIGHTON, (Fig. 7), and for synagogues, though for different reasons. Only rarely, as at Brighton, was the quality of workmanship combined with an imaginative use to produce something more than a coarse copy of the more conspicuous peculiarities of earlier styles.

At mid-century, a Baroque revival was the consequence of Louis Napoleon's scheme to modernize Paris along the lines initiated by Louis XIV. Because Paris was the centre of world fashions and its school of architecture, the Ecole des Beaux Arts, was the most influential in Europe, the Baroque spread widely. Not only did it serve as the background for the gaudy splendour of Napoleon III, but it was also the ideal style for the palaces of commerce, succeeding the relative restraint of the High Renaissance manner of the preceding generation. The OPÉRA, PARIS, by J. L. C. Garnier, built 1861-1874, (Fig. 8) stands for this revival at its most characteristic. A huge building at the head of an avenue leading down to the Louvre, its exterior is garnished with all manner of circular and oval windows, half-round and segmental arches, columns, pilasters and sculpture. It is more lavish of motifs than its Baroque models, yet the front, unlike a seventeenth-century façade, has no point of focus at the centre but distributes the emphasis evenly across the whole width. The spectacular nature of opera and its almost as showy audience had their counterpart in this building.

It was not as easy to find in the past a style suitable for more modern kinds of buildings, such as railway stations, warehouses and factories. Without a history themselves, such buildings were without an historic style; or if, as is the case of warehouses, there was an old tradition, it had never been graced with the label of art. The utility of the building, not its appearance, being the first consideration, new materials such as iron, steel, glass and cement were used by builder-engineers. These materials produced smooth surfaces and simple volumes, in contrast to the rest of nineteenth-century architecture. When these new elements were

Fig. 8: OPÉRA, *Paris. C. Garnier. 1861-1874—(Courtesy, The French Government Tourist Office).*

imaginatively used, there resulted a rare master-piece, prophetic of the twentieth century. In these cases, the functions of the designer and the engineer were in complete harmony of purpose.

The CRYSTAL PALACE, London, 1851, (Fig. 9), is the most memorable of these exceptions; a temporary large hall, it was built to shelter displays that were to be seen clearly by all. The times were auspicious for this new conception. Raised at the moment when British industrial enterprise was at the peak of its achievement, it was no wonder that the building was artistically successful. Designed by Joseph Paxton, who was not even an architect but one who had established his knowledge of glass and cast iron in the building of large greenhouses, the Crystal Palace was made of modern materials and assembled at great speed by a modern method of unit construction that employed unskilled crews. The formal characteristics of

modern architecture were present, a composition of clearly defined geometric volumes without the appearance of weight, and an interior space that through the glass extended into the park beyond. The Crystal Palace had many imitations; without fail, however, those imitations exhibited some traces of traditional styles grafted to the basic glass and iron essentials. The lessons of the building had gone unlearned.

For the Paris Exhibition of 1889, another landmark of modern architecture was erected, the EIFFEL TOWER (Fig. 2). That both the Crystal Palace and the Eiffel Tower were built for exhibitions is not surprising: to the Industrial Age an exhibition constituted a most stirring appeal to the imagination. The visitor went with a reverence not unlike that shown by mediaeval pilgrims to the holy places; they expected marvels. The Eiffel Tower was both a demonstration of the possibilities of steel construction and a call to modern man to leave

Fig. 9: CRYSTAL PALACE. *Sir Joseph Paxton. Built in London (England), for the Exhibition of 1851. Now destroyed—(From "Dickinsons Comprehensive Pictures of the Great Exhibition of 1851, painted by Messrs. Nash, Haghe and Roberts. Published by Dickinson Bros., 1854).*

the ground. A new dimension, that of great height, was being added to architecture, and a new sensation given to man. From the lofty viewing platform, one saw the horizon extending all around, and, detached from his footing on the ground, the viewer lost that control over his environment which depended upon his own presence as a key point in it. The Renaissance had come to an end. The Tower was the work not of an architect but of an engineer, Gustave Eiffel, who had come to know the possibilities of steel by building bridges. If it did not meet with the wide approval given the Crystal Palace a generation before, it was because the lines were now more sharply drawn between modernism and the traditional forms.

At the same time, in the United States, the design of buildings in height became the first real novelty in architecture in centuries. There had been high buildings before (the Pyramids for instance), but bulk had then been the first consideration. The Gothic cathedrals were also high, and afterwards height had been reserved expressly to suggest spiritual ends. Now height became a commercial advantage providing, as it did, more office space in central areas of great cities. What had been theoretically demonstrated by the Eiffel Tower was at the same time given useful application by private commercial enterprise. Chicago architects found the first solutions. By the mid 1890's, the technical problems were solved, and the perfection of the design followed immediately. Yet, at this moment, the development was arrested because skyscrapers with Gothic and Baroque overlay made their appearance. The nineteenth century closed on a still-unresolved issue—the education of a vast public and a majority of architects to a design without historic roots but developed within the requirements of modern materials and methods of construction.

9

Fig. 10: THE HAYWAIN. *John Constable. National Gallery, London. 1821.
50½″ x 70″—(Courtesy, The Trustees, The National Gallery of Art, London).*

Fig. 11: SELF-PORTRAIT. *Vincent Van Gogh. Wertheim Coll., Fogg Museum, Cambridge, Mass. 1888. 24½″ x 20½″—(Courtesy, The Fogg Art Museum, Harvard University, Wertheim Collection).*

Chapter II

PAINTING:
THE NINETEENTH CENTURY

Industrial and political revolution changed the course of painting as much as that of architecture. The old commissions were gone with the old patrons who had ordered frescoed ceilings and altarpieces for churches, portraits as records of family history, and sets of paintings to increase the splendour of the background against which their lives were passed. The new patron might buy old masters or the works of the more conservative painters. If he were more experienced, or connected by literary or political ties to radical movements, he might buy from the young artists. There were few in this second category. From the 1820's on, there was a strong cleavage among artists as between conservatives and progressives, the former favoured by governments and the wealthy, the latter favoured by nobody. Released from the demands of society, the progressives followed their own

interests, suffered often from a poverty which isolated them still further, frequented the company of fellow outcasts, and ended often by becoming eccentrics or revolutionaries. Not all the blame, however, should be laid at the door of an indifferent or hostile society: the painter in particular had, since the time of Leonardo da Vinci, claimed more and more a special status. From craftsman he had become creator: he was not prepared to surrender his liberty to paint as he wished. The nineteenth century ended with the gap still widening to the point where some artists, feeling totally abandoned or completely in opposition to society, resorted to suicidally violent courses of action.

In three countries at the time of the French Revolution there were powerful artistic movements in painting—movements that in large measure differed from one another. In Spain

Fig. 12: OATH OF THE HORATII. *J. L. David. Louvre, Paris. 1784. 11′ x 13′3″—*
(Courtesy, Alinari-Art Reference Bureau).

Goya followed an independent course out of the Rococo to a position where he might be compared with French painters of a generation later than himself. In England, the portrait tradition crumbled, and the painting of landscape took its place with such a concentration of effort that it anticipated French landscape painting of a half century later. Yet for the most part, from the 1780's to the present, French painting has influenced that of Europe and the Americas; it is therefore necessary to lay stress on its development, though it offers by no means the whole story.

Neo-classicism

In France, the artistic revolution was proclaimed by J. L. David (1748-1825) in the OATH OF THE HORATII (Fig. 12) painted in 1784 while he was a pupil of the French School in Rome. The very large canvas describes the solemn oath taken by three Roman brothers to fight the champions of their enemies, the Albans, even though their opponents were related to them through marriage. The story was familiar to all who were playgoers, as it was the theme of a famous French tragedy; and they could easily recognize in the picture the suggestion that the comforts and pleasure, even the happiness, of private life must be subordinated to the good of the state. For the politically minded it was a direct challenge to the self-indulgent royal government of Louis XVI.

The manner of the telling is as revolutionary as the matter. There are three distinct groups set on a shallow stage in front of and parallel to a simple arcade, one arch of which is allocated to each group. The figures are modelled to look as solid as statues, the details of dress and body rendered with some historical exact-

Fig. 13: DEATH OF SOCRATES. *J. L. David. Metropolitan Museum, New York. 1787. 59" x 78"—(Courtesy, Metropolitan Museum of Art. Wolfe Fund, 1931).*

ness. The artist was striving to attain in painting an equivalent to antique relief sculpture.

Three years later David repeated a political theme in the DEATH OF SOCRATES, (Fig. 13) using a similar shallow composition and again giving careful attention to archaeological detail. This treatment, too, exalted patriotism. In the fever of the next decades, however, these veiled suggestions of action were replaced by the more stimulating record of the events themselves. In this course, David was following an initiative already taken in England by American artists like Copley and West (Fig. 109, 115). David, himself an enthusiastic republican, was commissioned by the Assembly to paint a commemorative DEATH OF MARAT (Fig. 14) to honour a political martyr. It is the first painting since Velásquez' SURRENDER OF BREDA (see Book II, Fig. 118) to convey the impression of being a unique event, factual and unposed. Marat had been killed by a political opponent, Charlotte Corday, while in a special tub in which the state of his health required him to sit even when he was working. Within three days of the assassination, David visited the scene to obtain accurate detail—he had known Marat well. There is a total absence of stage heroics, of weeping spectators, of signs of violence. In their place are the tell-tale objects that can be observed as evidence: the knife, the quill pen, ink bottles and scraps of paper on which he had been working, the letter from the murderer asking him for an interview, the curious tub with its table top and the rude box beside it, the soft body displaying the small fatal wound. All of these details are lit as if by an artificially sharp light focused on each part separately for the purpose of precise

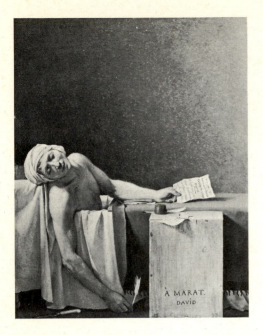

Fig. 14: DEATH OF MARAT. *J. L. David.*
Royal Museum of Fine Arts, Brussels.
1793. 65″ x 50½″—(Courtesy, Musées
Royaux des Beaux-Arts de Belgique).

her hair is bound by a simple classic fillet and her feet are bare like those of Greek maidens painted on a red-figured vase. The composition is a series of forms set parallel to the picture frame in a sequence of separate planes before a neutral brown background silhouetting these forms to best advantage. In pose it is a most unusual portrait, for the lady has her back to the spectator, the better to show the grace of her reclining figure and the complete ease of her manner. The face which she turns to us is completely placid though alert; but what we know of this relaxed and confident person we must learn through observation of her whole body, from head to tip of toe. This is very close indeed to the Greek conception of personality, and very far from the domination that the face had enjoyed ever since it had been looked upon as the outward sign of man's soul, and its irregularities the mark of his individuality.

When David fled from France on the return of the monarchy, he left disciples to continue his rather contradictory combination of classic imitation and exact observation. The best of these was Ingres (1780-1867). Whereas David was the innovator of his time, his followers became the conservatives, with Ingres their leader. The antique was still an ideal; yet it was no longer the statuesque which was admired but the linear grace of Greek vases; and the firm moral tone of David's early work gave way to the search for ideal beauty, as in Ingres' JUPITER AND THETIS (Fig. 16). The contrast between the solid muscularity of Jupiter and the fragile grace of Thetis is deliberate: each looks the more nearly perfect of a type by comparison with the opposite. By classic standards the result is an exaggeration and a disharmony which no sprinkling of the picture with ornamental antique details can conceal. The artist has not explored the theme for whatever feeling can be drawn from Thetis' appeal on behalf of her son Achilles; more important to Ingres were the sinuous curves of throat, back, arm, and arched foot of the woman, or the weight of the planted foot, the massive torso, and the spear-supported arm of Jupiter.

observation. Whereas art had formerly been used to ennoble fact, to comment upon it, or to arouse support, art here merely clarifies the details, shocks—and leaves the viewer to make up his own mind, or remain bewildered. It is the first step on the road to the candid camera.

David remained for nearly thirty years the leader of French art. Moreover, his talents were not limited to painting; for he designed interior decorations, furniture, and even women's fashions. He became pageant master to the infant republic; thereafter, as Napoleon's favourite painter, he was called upon to depict the imperial grandeur of the master of continental Europe.

The portrait of MADAME RÉCAMIER, 1800, (Fig. 15) a leading personality in literary society, mirrors the world over which David held sway. The evidence of fashionable Neo-Classicism is to be found in the lamp and settee, designed after furniture seen in Pompeian frescoes or recovered in excavations. Madame Récamier's dress is a modern adaptation of Greek costume,

Fig. 15: Mme. Récamier. *J. L. David. Louvre, Paris. 1800. 68″ x 96″—(Courtesy, The Louvre, Paris).*

Fig. 16: Jupiter and Thetis. *J. A. D. Ingres. Musée Granet, Aix-en-Provence. 1811. 130″ x 101″—(Courtesy, Bulloz-Art Reference Bureau).*

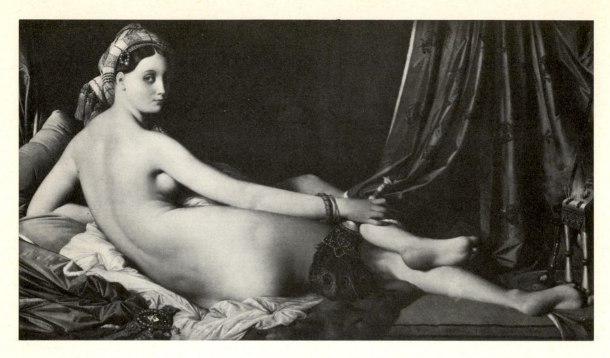

Fig. 17: ODALISQUE. *J. A. D. Ingres. Louvre, Paris. 1814. 36″ x 64″—(Courtesy, Alinari-Art Reference Bureau).*

The most complete statement of Ingres' ideal of feminine grace is to be seen in his several ODALISQUES (Fig. 17). The name is that given to the women of the Turkish harem, the mysteries of which were of romantic interest to the French of the time. The pose was chosen by Ingres to emphasize the extreme linear grace of the back, neck, legs and arms where none of the members is under any strain to support the body. If the woman were standing, the silhouette and contour lines of the body would be disturbed by the supporting structure of the bones beneath. The perfect smoothness of the surface of the body is contrasted to a surrounding wealth of rather fussy details—fan, jewellery, draperies, etc., very exactly described. That such perfection needs no special spark of humanity let alone individuality is made clear by the empty expressionless features of the ODALISQUE.

By contrast the features of MADAME RÉCAMIER by David indicate a personality.

When he abandoned the pursuit of ideal beauty exemplified by the ODALISQUES, and concentrated on the careful record of appearance Ingres was, however, the greatest portrait painter of his time. His clientele were the noble, the prosperous and the reactionary, and for them he felt the sympathy of the conservative. It was no accident that photography was invented in 1832 and that its first, and for a long time chief use was in taking portraits. Ingres' painting of MONSIEUR BERTIN, (Fig. 15) the newspaper editor, looks like a portrait produced in daguerreotype; in fact, it is almost the same in appearance, for Ingres did not consider colour an important element. The portrait is a statement of a kind of power that neither leans on external authority nor has need of pomp. Where formerly martial dress or kingly robes, ample curtains or great arches expanded the human gesture and related the individual to the source of his importance, M. Bertin in plain, drab male attire asserts his own importance, crowding the frame, one elbow thrust at the spectator in ruthless self-assertion.

Romanticism

A different viewpoint is represented by a series of painters who bear the label of Romantics in opposition to the Neo-Classicists of the Ingres school. This opposition did not appear until after the Napoleonic period; it was fostered by critics and especially by Ingres himself. It represented to some extent the split between conservatives and radicals in the fields of politics and ideas. The Neo-Classic vs. Romantic debate which ended with the 1860's, was also a revival of the late seventeenth-century argument between the form conceived in line (Poussin) and as constructed in colour (Rubens).

Far from constituting merely an effort to give ideal grace and beauty to the human form, art was to the Romantics an attempt to capture in paint the deep feelings that move men and at the same time provide them with an understanding that rational contemplation alone will not achieve. The Romantic painter himself, as well as his audience, is directly connected with what is represented in the painting. He chooses the distant and strange, the remote in time, the violent and painful, delivering his audience over to an imaginary world far more exciting than humdrum life.

The career of Géricault (1791-1824) is so strangely parallel to that of the English poets Shelley and Byron, who were his contemporaries, that it is obvious that his attitude was neither that of the French alone nor that of the painter only; rather, it represents a state of

Fig. 18: M. Bertin. *J. A. D. Ingres. Louvre, Paris. 1832. 46" x 37½" —(Courtesy, Alinari-Art Reference Bureau).*

Fig. 19: THE RAFT OF THE "MEDUSA". *T. Géricault. Louvre, Paris. 1818-1819.*
16′1″ x 23′6″—(Courtesy, The Louvre, Paris).

mind general among young spirits reacting against the dullness which the mass of Europeans welcomed after the wars. A wealthy young man in search of excitement, as happy racing horses as painting them, he was a fiery critic of the government, living violently and dying young. The RAFT OF THE MEDUSA (Fig. 19) describes the horrifying consequence of official incompetence revealed when a group of men were callously abandoned by their officers and left to float about in the South Atlantic. The painting is in the tradition of the OATH OF THE HORATII (Fig. 12), being of an immense eye-catching size; but whereas the earlier painting conveyed its message in the most direct and clearest of terms, the RAFT OF THE MEDUSA arouses a reaction by the turbulence of its composition. The spectator seems to overtake the raft from the left as it plunges in a choppy sea towards the distant hope of a sail on the horizon. His attention picks its way forward over a mass of bodies, dead, dying, and in despair; and these figures he knows better than those of the violently hopeful whose backs alone are seen against the stormy sky. Everywhere there are ragged shapes, sharp contrasts of light and dark, even the conflict of direction of hope, left to right, and of wind, right to left. It was not Géricault's intention, however, to sacrifice truth of incident to effect, but to make truth a moving experience; for he questioned survivors and made trips to the Paris morgue the better to record the appearance of the dead.

The other great Romantic French painter is Eugène Delacroix (1798-1863). Though Delacroix lived an outwardly more peaceful life than Géricault he sought just as diligently for the unusual in the course of his travels to England, the Netherlands and Algeria. He never visited Italy, the goal of more conventional artists. His model amongst painters was Rubens whose gusto and great painterly powers he admired and imitated. Almost without exception his choice of subject was a stirring event in times past, some strange scene in the present or an occasion of violence. The commonplace appeared only in his rare studies of still life; and, as for portraiture, he confined himself to a few portraits of friends.

The MASSACRE AT SCIO, 1824, (Fig. 20) commemorates the Greek War of Liberation, a struggle which had engaged the sympathies of Byron as well. The brutality of the Turks to all the Greeks is symbolized by this collection of sufferers male and female, combatant and non-combatant, young and old. The victims are composed in two loosely related groups which open to show the battlefield as a distant landscape. Like West's DEATH OF WOLFE (Fig. 115), the painting is a posed summary rather than a simple record of the event. Its appeal is less to the reflective imagination, however, than directly to the feelings of alarm, pity and horror. There is the disturbing factor of two focuses of attention, at left and right of the canvas. Light and shadow playing across the colourful mass conveys the impression of change. A wide range of colours and textures of flesh and garment, often juxtaposed in strongly contrasting pairs excite the senses. The obvious acts of violence represented in the Massacre are hardly more disturbing than the use Delacroix made of design to express his emotions and catch those of the spectator.

It is recorded that Delacroix made fundamental changes in this canvas after seeing Constable's HAYWAIN (Fig. 10) which was exhibited in 1824 in Paris.

Fig. 20: MASSACRE AT SCIO. E. Delacroix. Louvre, Paris. 1824. 13'10" x 11'7"—(Courtesy, Archives Photographiques).

Fig. 21: PORTRAIT OF CHOPIN. *E. Delacroix. Louvre, Paris. 1838. 18″ x 15″—(Courtesy, Bulloz-Art Reference Bureau).*

As he matured Delacroix's manner of painting became a more effective vehicle. His ABDUCTION OF REBECCA (Colour Plate II), an episode from the novel *Ivanhoe* by Sir Walter Scott—as great a favourite of European readers as he was of English—is an act of violence cast in a distant time, the Middle Ages. The action which is form in motion, hints at more than one can surely see and at actions still to come. Unlike Ingres, who paid close attention to linear directions and careful studio lighting, Delacroix described form through light and shadow relationships revealed in a wide range of colour. The suggestion of contrasting or reflected colours in shadows, the mutual strengthening of complementary colours, indeed, the employment of every device that can represent light as it appears to us as colour—all such possibilities were explored by Delacroix.

The portraits Delacroix painted were those of friends with whom he shared a deep sympathy. FREDERICK CHOPIN (Fig. 21) was a stormy personality and the representative of a nation, Poland, that was struggling against Russian oppression. His head half turned away and slightly bent betrays a painful concentration on something that has made him oblivious to the spectator. It may be the tortures of concentration as he sits composing at the piano. A dark and turbulent background seems to half envelop the head, leaving much of his person a mystery to us. So interpreted, Chopin is a model of the misunderstood and suffering genius, and the very opposite to the exactly described, confident and aggressive M. BERTIN (Fig. 18) by Ingres painted in the same decade.

Today, Delacroix's choice of subjects, exhibiting as they do a romantic taste for violence, has made him seem more out of date than most nineteenth-century painters. At the same time, his concern with colour, extending as it did to the first essays into the field of a scientific theory of light, places him a generation ahead of contemporary French painters. The adaptation of a theory of light to practical ends in colour composition is his lasting contribution to the art of painting, a contribution freely admired by the generation that followed him.

As a young man Delacroix had continued the tradition of painting history with a political intent; thus, the MASSACRE AT SCIO is a poignant record of the brutalities of the war of Greek Independence. Again, after the rejection of the Bourbons in 1830, he painted *Liberty at the Barricades*. Subsequently both he and the whole group of Neo-Classicists concentrated on themes entirely removed from the contemporary scene or commonplace life.

Nevertheless, these themes were not completely neglected, however unpopular they were in those circles which had taken flight from democracy after the unsettling experience of the French Revolution. The forerunner of those who were to make the state of the contemporary world the theme of art was Goya (1747-1828), a Spanish artist somewhat cut off from the general European development. A court painter

Fig. 22: FAMILY OF CHARLES IV. *F. Goya. Prado, Madrid. 1800. 9′2″ x 11′—*
(Courtesy, Anderson-Art Reference Bureau).

commissioned to create the decorative frivolities that were the business of such men as Tiepolo, or to paint the portraits of the sadly dilapidated Spanish aristocracy, he was able, without incurring the displeasure of his patrons, to perform the mystifying feat of depicting the traditional pageantry of royalty performed by creatures as empty of the dignity of their station as puppets moved by strings.

Social Realism

The FAMILY OF CHARLES IV (Fig. 22) is a group portrait obviously in imitation of Velásquez' MAIDS OF HONOUR (Book II, Fig 119); for Goya himself is to be seen in the background at the left working on a great canvas. The large painting is drenched with the rich colour of costumes, many of which are adorned with bright sashes of knightly orders or twinkling with a display of medals and jewels. The very brilliance of the effect tends to conceal the substance of what is at the best a rather pathetic group; indeed, the most impressive thing about them is their clothes. They are only the ghosts of monarchs, as Napoleon's invasion of Spain proved.

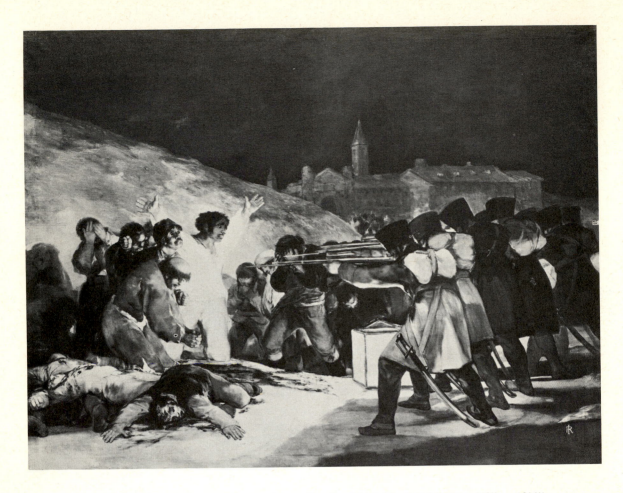

Fig. 23: THE THIRD OF MAY. *F. Goya. Prado, Madrid. 1814-1815 . 8'9" x 13'4"—* *(Courtesy, Anderson-Art Reference Bureau).*

Of the national uprising that followed, Goya had much to say. A series of prints in aquatint, the *Disasters of the War*, describes the barbarities practised by both sides. There is not a trace of patriotism in the prints, and few indications of the virtues that are supposed to ennoble war. His criticism can be summed up in a painting, the THIRD OF MAY 1808, (Fig. 23) done in 1814 to commemorate the unsuccessful rising of the citizens of Madrid in 1808. The execution of a group of patriots by a French firing squad might have been presented as the occasion for a grand, heroic gesture. It was not so treated. The firing squad and its victims are held together by the light radiating on them from a great lantern; beyond them the night is a wall of silence. A baroque compositional device, such a central light had hitherto been employed as a sign of at least temporary unity; but Goya has made a mockery of the friendly light. The victims are a disordered mass individually portraying every reaction except heroism; and the soldiers are not even villains, but the machinelike agents of destruction. Goya's manner of painting in broad areas of colour applied in great splashes of paint suggests the haste of an observer and the rapid passing of the event observed. This impression, together

Fig. 24: BOBALICON (*The Big Booby*). *F. Goya. c.1818. Aquatint etching—*
(Courtesy, Metropolitan Museum of Art. Dick Fund, 1924).

with the absence of all traditional contrivance, gives to the painting the ring of authentic evidence attesting to the stupidity and degradation of war. Comparison with the DEATH OF WOLFE by Benjamin West (see Fig. 115 and text, page 108) will disclose how modern Goya is in his attitude.

Man's foolishness became only too apparent to Goya in his later years. Thus, in another set of aquatints, *The Absurdities*, Goya employed the imagery of nightmare to describe the mad state of the world. For all their inscriptions, the prints cannot be exactly interpreted; but their general intention can be felt. The one labelled BOBALICON (The Big Booby) (Fig. 24) is of a great lout dancing madly about to the accompaniment of witches' screamings while a man and woman cringe before them. The blotlike shading of the medium of aquatint has the look of thick fog, and is the very atmosphere of fear.

Because *The Absurdities* are portrayed in Goya's private language—a medium of communication that we can only approximately understand—they are remarkably similar to much modern art, which, too, is often based on the language of dreams.

Goya's increasing pessimism is nevertheless evidence of the artist's abiding interest in, and preoccupation with man. Otherwise, why would he have resorted to the medium of the printed page with its possibility of wider distribution? The other great graphic artist of the nineteenth century was also a commentator on society, the French lithographer Honoré Daumier (1808-1879). Working for a succession of newspapers as a cartoonist and as an illustrator of books, he began as a liberal critic of the government; then, after a time spent in gaol, he switched to the safer field of satirical comment on human nature and returned to the political sphere only at the end of his life. LE VENTRE LÉGISLATIF, 1834, (Fig. 25) is a biting attack on the corruption and stupidity of the

23

Fig. 25: LE VENTRE LÉGISLATIF. *H. Daumier. 1834. Lithograph—(Courtesy, Metropolitan Museum of Art. Rogers Fund, 1920).*

government of the day. The gallery of four tiers of caricatures is kept just short of monotony by variations in the pattern of black and white; but these monsters would seem hardly human enough to be menacing were it not for the single standing figure of one of their number in the foreground, whose position before the curving white rail thrusts him into the company of those who look at the lithograph. This man's corpulence can be measured because his figure is presented in a diagonal position, a position defined by the white rail on which he leans heavily; moreover, unlike his fellow, he is hardly a caricature at all. This "Rogues' Gallery" comes to life whenever we look at it, for we see every last monster in it, together with the

man before the rail, at the same time. He introduces us into the company of the politically corrupt, and is a bridge between the viewer and the grotesque embodiments of evil.

Caricature has no value if it does not appeal to wide sections of the public; indeed, its message is short lived if it does not deal with basic human characteristics that reveal themselves from one generation to another. LE VENTRE LÉGISLATIF was not only directed against a specific set of corrupt politicians, each of whom is recognizable behind the exaggerations; it applied also to *all* dishonest political figures. When Daumier turned to the world around him, his criticism embraced a much wider range and was not so bitterly expressed, excep-

Fig. 26: THE THIRD CLASS CARRIAGE. *H. Daumier. Metropolitan Museum of Art, New York. c.1860-1870. 26" x 35½"—(Courtesy, The Metropolitan Museum of Art. Bequest of Mrs. H. O. Havemeyer, 1929. The H. O. Havemeyer Collection).*

tion being made for all those having to do with the administration of justice. The THIRD-CLASS CARRIAGE (Fig. 26) is a little world in itself, isolated for the moment; and yet it is a miniature of the whole of society. On the foremost bench is a group representing the family from infancy to old age; all of its members are silent, wrapped in their own thoughts. Beyond are benches of animated conversationalists representing a variety of people engaged in the give and take of man as a social creature; the railway carriage is a cross-section of the world of Daumier's middle-class experience.

The THIRD CLASS CARRIAGE is a painting, one of many that Daumier made but which were not exhibited during his lifetime. They

are without the bite of his political cartoons, the humour of his social criticisms. In this painting the figures are given short proportions, are modelled to suggest weight, and emerge out of the shadows clothed in the most sombre tones. If the result is a little depressing, it is because Daumier, through the eyes of a liberal, saw France as a discouraging place for plain people. It was quite another France which glittered at the Opéra in Paris.

Daumier's graphic output was too narrowly French in its subject matter to be immediately known outside his native land; but the work of Jean François Millet (1814-1875) gave wider appeal to the social genre. His *Angelus, Sower,* and GLEANERS are among the best-known paint-

Fig. 27: THE GLEANERS. *J. F. Millet. Louvre, Paris. 1857. 33" x 44"—(Courtesy, Alinari-Art Reference Bureau).*

ings of the nineteenth century. The GLEANERS (Fig. 27) presents a scene of thrifty peasants gathering stray grain stalks from the fields after harvesting. The bent bodies of the women stand out in sharp contrast to the graceful forms of Ingres or the sensuous vitality of Delacroix. The placing of the women close together, as well as the synchronizing of their action, suggests a stately sequence of movement taking place isolated and clear against the monotony of an extremely bare setting. The three are united to this setting by the repetition of rhythm in the stacks and in the rounded hay wagon of the middleground. The stooping women are heavily modelled by shadow against a light ground. Millet's achievement in this treatment of the GLEANERS inspired an unusual admiration among sculptors in both Europe and America. The enormous success of his paintings can be traced to the high esteem in which honest labour and simple piety were held by the later nineteenth-century public. His almost complete fall in our estimation today is due to our recognition that the world is not governed by such simple virtues. Daumier as a moralist represented a more complicated world—a world much closer to our own.

Another who made social genre his special theme was Gustave Courbet (1819-1877). It was his temperament to be a rebel against both Neo-

Fig. 28: THE STONE BREAKERS. *G. Courbet. Formerly State Picture Gallery, Dresden (destroyed?). 1849. 63" x 102"—(Courtesy, Marburg-Art Reference Bureau).*

Classicists and Romantics, fighting his battles with officialdom on behalf of his choice of subjects. Courbet's statement, "Show me an angel and I will paint one", summed up his position; what he saw was all that he would paint. The STONE BREAKERS (Fig. 28) will illustrate what he meant. An old man and a boy are absorbed in work, their backs turned to the spectator. With impartial care the painter has described each stone, the dress, the tools, the other equipment; it has all been done with the objectivity of a camera and without any special focus of attention at any one point. Indeed, in a black-and-white reproduction it looks like a photograph, save that no photograph of the time or for long afterwards could render so sensuously the texture of materials. The latter are a major concern of Courbet's—the metal lunch pail, the wooden and the coarse leather shoes, the different types of cloth, and the rocks themselves, some fresh-split and dusty, others still lichen-stained. Where everything is

equally important to the senses, nothing can be emphasized.

Painted in 1849 at the height of the reaction from the political disturbances caused by the radical socialists, the STONE BREAKERS was attacked as both vulgar and dangerous. Certainly it did not place labour in a noble light the way Millet had represented it; but neither did it suggest the oppression of the poor from youth to old age. Courbet welcomed the attack, however, and in both his art and his public career he continued the socialist pose. Nonetheless, his real interests did not lie in social propaganda but in the painting of nudes, flower pieces, and landscapes, none of which had any deeper meaning than the coarse colourful vitality that they exhibited. It was Courbet who re-introduced and perfected the use of the palette knife for applying paint in slathers—Rembrandt, whom he much admired, had also employed the same method—giving thereby the effect of great energy to his canvases.

Fig. 29: THE FIFE PLAYER. *E. Manet. Louvre, Paris. 1886. 63" x 38"—(Courtesy, Agraci- Art Reference Bureau).*

Although the next artistic generation which began in the 1860's came to maturity in the midst of political and social disturbance and was itself often of strong political conviction, it came right out for "art for art's sake", retaining at the same time Courbet's contention that nature itself and the visible world were the only source of material. Edouard Manet (1832-1883), the oldest of this generation, painted many group and single figures with little concern for what the subjects of his paintings were doing. His FIFER, (Fig. 29) is less portrait than still life. What has occupied the painter has been the pattern of colours transferred flat to the two dimensions of the canvas from his observation of it in life. The body casts almost no shadow, and what there is falls on a colour which is not only stood upon but also serves as background and, indeed, corresponds to no observable phenomena of nature but is really a foil for the blues and reds of the pattern.

Pre-Impressionist Landscape Painting

The middle of the nineteenth century finally saw landscape become the preferred theme of painting. The great concern with classic art which had marked the beginning of the century precluded landscape for which there were no antique models. In France it is only after 1825 that a real beginning is made. The same was not true of England, where there had been a heavy demand for landscape, in part satisfied by the purchase of paintings of the seventeenth century, in part by contemporary artists. The old masters supplied a taste for a generalized landscape; the new men were essentially topog-

Fig. 30: Snow Storm. *W. M. Turner. National Gallery, London. 1811. 36″ x 42″—(Courtesy, The Trustees, The National Gallery of Art, London).*

raphers, recording the appearance of famous cities, country houses, or historic monuments in their natural settings. The two requirements were combined in Turner (1775-1851), who throughout most of his career provided water colours for several series of engravings, such as the *Harbours of England*, while regularly exhibiting oil paintings of a less local nature. Even where the site was carefully indicated, Turner exaggerated the natural features, hills becoming precipices, and skies being filled with storm-torn clouds. He shared a widespread English taste for the awe-inspiring elements present in nature and, in the canvases, considerably emphasized by the artist's distortion.

Turner steadily moved towards the depiction of yet more violent natural effects. In the Snow Storm, (Fig. 30) for example, the ocean is raging, the air is full of snow, and the ship is all but lost from sight in the storm. The elements are so intermingled that water and air cannot be distinguished; in fact, the picture might well be hung upside down. Yet it is not a creation of pure fantasy: the atmospheric effects are as accurate as they are improbable, except in some natural catastrophe. This effect in painting landscape is the equivalent to the Romantic violence of Delacroix.

Another of Turner's paintings, Rain, Steam and Speed, 1844, (Fig. 31) the view of an on-

Fig. 31: RAIN, STEAM, SPEED. *W. M. Turner. National Gallery, London. 1844.
35¾″ x 48″—(Courtesy, The Trustees, The National Gallery of Art, London).*

rushing train crossing a bridge in a squall of
rain, is novel in theme with none of the heroics
customary to his work. A curtain of light dissolves the solid world, revealing the rain-filled
air and the turbulent components of the atmosphere. In this picture the four traditional
elements of the world unite—earth, water, air,
and fire—in an exhibition of energy to which
both nature and man contribute.

The second English landscapist of importance
was John Constable (1776-1837). The landscapes he chose were local and familiar, peaceful
and often cultivated—in contrast to the exotic,
horrendous, or panoramic themes sought by
Turner. Temperamentally, he was much closer
than Turner to the Dutch painters of the
seventeenth century; for the Essex landscape

that he preferred was low lying and watery, its
skies filled with clouds off the North Sea, as
in the Netherlands. Where Turner searched for
the unusual and exciting, Constable welcomed
the commonplace in nature.

WEYMOUTH BAY, 1816, (Fig. 32) was, exceptionally, painted on the south coast of England.
It is a vast seashore scene, advancing beyond
the Dutch landscapes of Van Goyen in the scale
of its conception. Two horizons, the one at left
by the shore, the other inland upon the downs
are joined by the crest of the hill over which
vanishes a train of clouds leading to the land
that lies beyond. The sky above is given shape
by the clouds, the land beneath is carefully laid
out in the changing colours of receding beaches,
meadows and scrub-covered hillside. In this

Fig. 32: WEYMOUTH BAY. *John Constable. National Gallery, London. 1816.*
29" x 21¼"—(Courtesy, The Trustees, The National Gallery of Art, London).

almost featureless panorama nothing holds the attention save space ordered by Constable's meticulous observation of the colour and shape of natural phenomena that fill it. Yet there is an air of permanence about WEYMOUTH BAY, as if it were a landscape illumined by a steady unchanging light. There is very little hint of change in it.

More and more he came to rely on small oil sketches made on the spot to record exact colourations of light at certain hours of the day. New and bold ways of applying paint without blending it carefully on the canvas were devised to approximate the vibration of light.

In black-and-white reproduction the HAY-WAIN (Fig. 10) is a remarkably dull great painting. There is no single interesting detail to be examined nor great panorama to be explored. In the actual painting, however, there is an unprecedented subtlety in the recording of light as it falls on the stream, through the trees, and upon the fields beyond; the effect is so right as to provide the impression of light-filled air itself.

STOKE-BY-NAYLAND, 1836, (Fig. 33) represents his latest manner. The flickering of light represented by innumerable brush strokes left unsmoothed upon the canvas obscures the precise form of objects which are seen as phenomena of light not as things in themselves. Constable's art has denied the importance of all that lies beyond what one sees at the moment. The accumulations of memory have been set aside in favour of the impression of the moment.

Fig. 33: STOKE-BY-NAYLAND. *John Constable. Art Institute, Chicago. 1836.*
49½″ x 66½″—(Courtesy, The Art Institute of Chicago, Mr. and Mrs. W. W.
Kimball Collection).

In almost every respect Constable anticipated the later French landscape painters. When his HAYWAIN was exhibited in France in 1824, it created a furor, was greatly admired by Delacroix, and along with other works done by him, helped launch French landscape painting of the middle and second half of the nineteenth century. That he, and even Turner to a lesser degree, should in this respect take precedence of the French is probably due to the essentially urban character of French art in the eighteenth century and to its patriotic tinge in the early nineteenth; it was, moreover, a time when the rural interests of the English gentry provided a market for landscape unparalleled in France.

The first of French landscapists of the nineteenth century was Camille Corot (1796-1875). Although he was an assiduous sketcher in pencil and oils of actual details of nature and of whole scenes, his seeing was not that of the camera but of a peculiarly selective vision. Most of his early paintings are of easily recognized places; more often than not they are panoramic in their scope, but of such a small scale that they are like acutely visualized memory images in which size is never a factor, time stands still, and the lighting or colouring that belongs to the time of day most pleasantly remembered illuminates every detail: bright sun in Rome, the greys and browns of twilight in the plateau of central

France, and the clear light of seashore at La Rochelle. Though he calls them "studies" for much larger canvases which were to be more like the ideal landscapes of the seventeenth century, they are in reality impressions in intention a little like Constable's sketches. Nevertheless, Corot stands outside the general trend represented by Turner and Constable—a trend followed by later painters who tried in their canvases to capture the changing process of nature.

Such is the view of CHARTRES (Fig. 34). This is much more than a portrait of the great church which would be more impressive seen from the south. Viewed from this angle the cathedral extends from the middle ground back to the horizon at the expense of a steep foreshortening that reduces the magnificence of the building. The two towers repeating the motif of two trees in the foreground complete the linking of the church to the rest of the landscape. Carefully described though the church is, there is as much care taken with the heap of stone in the front of the picture as if all Corot saw was equally important in his experience. Though there is a cool sunlight and clouds in the sky there is none of the display of the forces of nature to be seen in Constable or Turner.

Fig. 34: VIEW OF CHARTRES. *J. B. C. Corot. Louvre, Paris. c.1840. 24½" x 19¾"—(Courtesy, Art Reference Bureau).*

A whole group of French painters associated with Corot became established in the 1840's in the forest of Fontainebleau, southeast of Paris, at the village of Barbizon, from which they took their name. Théodore Rousseau is the best known among them. They, too, did much painting directly from nature. Their point of view was somewhat coloured by the Dutch painters Jacob Ruysdael and Hobbema; it was from the former in particular that they took the conception of nature as a contest of forces—the weather, trees, and rocky soil contending one against the other. This interpretation is more in harmony with the spirit of the nineteenth century than the dreamlike world of Corot. It was the age when rugged individualism, and the principle of every man for himself, provided the basic rules of behaviour. For quite some-time, however, those in the industrial age who had striven and succeeded, especially the wealthy picture buyers, preferred a kind of idyllic peace in the works of art that they purchased; for to them it represented an escape into a calm that they did not find in the world outside the picture frame. This accounts for the unrivalled popularity of Corot during the second half of the nineteenth century among conservative picture collectors.

Impressionism

By 1860, landscape was a major concern of French artists. Ingres and Delacroix were still alive, but their interests were outmoded and neither painted landscapes. Nor did Daumier: his strong social consciousness could not be channelled into fields or trees. Millet and Courbet, Corot, the Barbizon painters, and lesser men—all these were active in the forest of Fontainebleau, in the countryside around Paris, and at the mouth of the Seine near Le Havre where in summer they went to paint the sea. A new generation was emerging, the best of whose painters were for nearly two decades loosely associated—as much by opposition to conservatism as by common artistic beliefs—into a group known today as the Impressionists, a name given to them on the occasion of their first joint exhibition in 1874. To them reality

was embodied in change and not in static things known only after many observations.

Their purpose was to catch the effect of the moment, of life seen passing by, as a fragment of a changing scene. The few, mainly literary figures, who understood what the painters were trying to do brought forward the principle of Art for Art's Sake to defend their radical position. What an artist wished to paint was art to be understood without relation to subject represented or to any role the public might call upon painting to play, either as propaganda or as illustration. Because these artists were in the middle of the nineteenth century living at a time when scientific methods were being applied to everything, there was some talk among them of scientific colour systems to render the effects of light physically more accurate in the medium of paint. While discoveries in the laws of optics and of light stimulated experiments by the painters, the results could hardly be termed scientific, determined as they were not by machines for measurement but by the individual artist's choice.

The Impressionists were not a closed group. Though they can be listed by their participation in the eight Impressionist exhibitions, one of the most famous of their number, Manet, never sent a picture. The "Group" exhibition was the way new developments in art were to become known. In the previous century, painters had exhibited only at annual exhibitions. The public, and even the private, purchasers had slight indications of new developments; and the whole process must have seemed very gradual, and not at all alarming. Now changes occurred more conspicuously. A group of artists, each exhibiting several paintings, often tagged themselves, or were tagged, with a special name to aid identity. Eventually, either they or their friends put out a declaration of purpose or "manifesto" to explain their art. The exhibition became a method of advertising wares, the young painters being deprived of chances to exhibit in the great state shows or to sell to most collectors, their work being of too radical a nature for the conservative tastes of such

Fig. 35: THE RIVER. *C. Monet. Art Institute, Chicago. 1868. 35⅞″ x 39½″—* *(Courtesy, The Art Institute of Chicago. Potter Palmer Collection).*

collectors. Because the sales at these group exhibitions were usually very small the chief advantage and purpose was self-justification. Since the mid-nineteenth century the group exhibition has continued to emphasize change as a sequence of revolutions, each calling forth the violent opposition of antagonists and the exaggerated support of adherents. Born of the extreme isolation of the artist in the nineteenth and in the first half of the twentieth century, when only the group exhibition offered him comfort and public notice, the need is today slowly receding as the gulf between artist and public narrows.

Among the Impressionists, the landscapists

were Pissarro (1831-1903), Monet (1840-1926), and Sisley (1839-1899); Manet (1832-1883) and Degas (1834-1917) were the genre and still-life painters; Renoir (1841-1919) belonged to both groups. The Impressionist landscape was the product of developments going back to the English painters of the first third of the century. Its characteristics may be seen developing in THE RIVER, (Fig. 35) 1868 by Monet. From the distant roofs of houses to the straw hat at the front, forms are suggested by areas of colour, not by detailed modelling. Cast shadows are made colourful with the complementary tones. What is represented is reduced to what immediately meets the eye before lengthy examination supplies further details. It is a landscape without strong attractions to explore in depth. The spectator is content to revel in the sun-drenched colour.

The passion to put down the exact colouration of light impelled artists to explore the variations of time and place, the different hours of the day, the times of fog, or when smoke or steam filled the air. Occasionally they attempted the effect of snow upon the ground, more often the light in the vicinity of water. Such careful observation had been inaugurated by Constable; but most of the notes he took in the form of sketches were transposed to larger canvases in his studio. Monet attempted to finish large canvases on the spot simplifying his compositions to save time so that he could concentrate on his recording of the colour of light before it changed.

Such a painting is THE CLIFF AT ETRETAT, 1886, (Colour Plate VI) which shows part of a sea cliff on the English Channel; a natural bridge has a special interest as a curiosity, but this Monet has not exploited. There is nothing of topographical interest, nor even as much elaboration of composition into depth as can be encountered in his earlier landscapes. Not even the height is given, cut off as the rock is by the frame.

His whole interest has been light. The artist has been at great pains to describe the infinite variety of the play of light, whether direct or reflected off chalk cliffs or water. This effect he has achieved as a result of careful observation born of years of experience and by means of a manner of painting in which each patch of light is broken down into many small dabs of pigment. For a given area one colour predominates; but laid beside it are other colours that represent

Fig. 36: WATER LILIES, GIVERNY. *C. Monet. Museum of Modern Art, New York. c.1920. 6'6½" x 19'7½"—(Collection, The Museum of Modern Art, New York. Mrs. Simon Guggenheim Fund).*

Fig. 37: BOULEVARD DES ITALIENS, MORNING SUNLIGHT. *C. Pissarro. 1897—* *(Courtesy, National Gallery of Art, Washington, D.C. Chester Dale Collection.)*

reflected light from other coloured surfaces; or the complementary of the basic colour is put beside it to heighten the intensity of the basic; or two colours are simply juxtaposed so that when seen at a distance they mingle to form the desired colour. In this texture of colours there is no stability of effect, but only a vibration of rapidly succeeding impressions made up of colour-mixes. The light reflected from the cliff, not the cliff itself, is recorded; and the intensity of this visual impression blots out the slowly accumulated knowledge of cliffs and rocks which the spectator has gathered in the past. Yet this truth of the moment is a limited vision; for

the artist must work rapidly, on the spot, and, ideally, he must complete the canvas at one sitting. No elaborate compositional schemes are possible when time is so precious to the painter. For that matter there is no place in instantaneous vision for thoughtful compositions.

The process was to go much further with Monet. WATER LILIES, GIVERNY, 1907, (Fig. 36) seen as a shimmer of colour into which the other physical characteristics of the things represented have all but disappeared. It is only one step further to pure abstraction when nothing but areas of colour reflect light back from the canvas to the viewer.

Fig. 38: MOULIN DE LA GALETTE. *A. Renoir. Louvre, Paris. 1876. 51½″ x 69″—*
(Courtesy, Bulloz-Art Reference Bureau).

Other landscape painters were not prepared to go as far. Camille Pissarro, (1830-1903), preserved the structure of forms seen in space, and usually his works have a recognizable location. BOULEVARD DES ITALIENS, MORNING SUNLIGHT (Fig. 37) wherein the light of early morning is studied against the blur of a busy city has all the authenticity of a casual glance from a hotel window.

Landscape was not the only area in which Impressionist painters could pursue their studies. Renoir repeatedly described groups and single figures splashed over by light falling through the trees upon them. The MOULIN DE LA GALETTE, 1876 (Fig. 38) is checkered with lights falling on the crowded scene. The eye dances from high light to high light, from the man's shoes and trouser at the left to the girl

in the middle ground, to the straw hats, to the glasses on the table and to the shoulder of the girl in the front centre. Here and there on flesh and dress are reflected lights shot up from brighter surfaces. Light is everywhere, even in the sombre dress of the men. It imparts gaiety to the scene, it gives buoyancy to the merriment and it dissolves much of the feeling of weight and mass in the single figures. The MOULIN DE LA GALETTE is the impression of a moment, however; the lights will change and a fresh impression will be given.

Impressionist landscape has left important legacies: an awareness of the richness of colour in nature and a tolerance of its brighter hues. These attitudes have survived the disappearance of Impressionism itself.

Fig. 39: BAR AT THE FOLIES-BERGÈRES. *E. Manet. The Courtauld Collection, London. 1881-1882. 37½" x 51"—(Courtesy, Art Reference Bureau).*

The interest in light was not confined to natural illumination. Manet's A BAR AT THE FOLIES-BERGÈRES (Fig. 39) is an astonishing display of the effect of artificial light on all manner of coloured objects composed of widely varying materials and textures; some objects are opaque, others are transparent, and some are visible only as reflections of their images mirrored on the wall behind the bar. The light, which is everywhere, unites the many details. The choice of subject is characteristic of the Impressionists: an event of ordinary life in which the spectator is intimately involved. Indeed, it is the spectator's world that is reflected in the mirror; for he may be actually present in the person of the top-hatted man who stands giving his order to the girl. Yet to the man at the bar whose focus of interest and clear vision is reserved to the face of the girl, the mirror with its world is a little blurred. This is the purest, most mechanical way of seeing, like that of the eye of the camera with its limited depth of focus. Furthermore, a close examination of the goblet with roses reveals that glass, water and flowers dissolve into dashes of paint which assume form only when seen at a distance. In a sense, the spectator completes the picture by searching out the proper distance he must stand from it. But if he is the top-hatted gentleman, the goblet and flowers, on the edge of his vision and interest, remain shapeless colours and out of focus.

Fig. 40: Prima Ballerina. E. Degas. Louvre, Paris. c.1876. 23″ x 16½″. Pastel —(Courtesy, Bulloz-Art Reference Bureau).

The work of Degas shows less concern with light; indeed, unlike the other Impressionists, he almost never painted out-of-doors; and he had a deep reverence for the past. Yet he was as contemporary as the others in his desire to record the momentary. The Prima Ballerina (Fig. 40) is seen from a loge towards which she is looking. The painting seems extensible in several directions, not only towards the sides and back, but upwards as well. The eye sweeping across the stage is not fixed as it would be were the ballerina in mid-stage; instead, it by-passes her. She herself is seen as delicately poised on one foot and grotesquely foreshortened — the very essence of what is seen, not what is known to be.

The angled view from above had been adopted by the Japanese as a means of obtaining a detached viewpoint from which to watch the passing scene. Though this device became known in western Europe in the 1850's, it was Degas in particular who used it to best effect. Of the importations that, during the next hundred years, were to take the place of perspective conventions of Renaissance origin, this was the first.

The Glass of Absinthe, (Fig. 41) 1876 is one of the clearest examples of this indebtedness. Everything is represented diagonally to the picture plane that cuts abruptly across the table in front from which the viewer has just risen to glance across at the man and woman. In this moment of observation he is only interested in the heads of the pair opposite, and the edges of his vision are blurred. Of course one can, with leisure, fill in the details of setting; but Degas along with the other Impressionists preferred this sudden revelation as giving a glimpse into life which no posed composition could give.

By the end of his career Degas had completely replaced the set piece by the accidental. THE TUB (Fig. 42) is a female nude; but it is not like any that had gone before. The woman's body is crouched down in such a way as to conceal the traditional beautiful contours of the female body; and she is engaged, not in the graceful act of holding a jug or fastening her sandal, but in washing her neck.

All the accessories of the bath are conspicuous and important; in fact, a third of the picture is taken up with the table and its contents. So extraordinary is the angle of view that it all but destroys our judgment; our conventional notion of the external world as presented to us in a head-on view, our method of apprehending it from a repeated viewing of it frontally, has not fitted us to decide whether the anatomy revealed in this picture is accurately drawn or whether the pitchers are presented properly foreshortened. Manet had pointed out that we do not see what we think we do; Degas has shown just as clearly that we are not sure of any but customary views. And Monet's cliffs are stone dissolved into a shimmer of light, a contradiction of common sense.

Fig. 41: THE GLASS OF ABSINTHE. E. Degas. The Louvre, Paris. 1876. 36″ x 27″—(Courtesy, Agraci-Art Reference Bureau).

For a while these revelations were exciting. Visual perception was sharpened and the innumerable possibilities of seeing were explored: the whole material world was there for the painting. Accordingly, the Impressionists' paintings are packed with vitality—the beating light of the sun, the glimmer of artificial light on coloured glass, the light movement of dancers, the physical concentration of Degas' bather at her task. Ultimately, however, artists, among them some of the Impressionists, questioned the goal of an art that avoided all emphasis or comment. Merely being sharply aware of the moment of life was not enough. Thus, about 1885, there set in a strong reaction to Impressionism; and though its vogue lingered on in provincial imitations and modifications well into the twentieth century, as a leading force it passed away leaving European art with a brighter colour sense.

Post Impressionism

Two directions of development were taken by painters at the end of the century. On the one hand they were more interested in design than in observation, looking rather at the canvas than at nature. On the other they were using their art to give their personal comment on life. Where the Impressionists had assumed a benevolent neutrality towards society, the new generation was always critical and usually hostile. This attitude was not confined to artists alone; for the age was one of political radicalism as well when it was held that only by violent revolution could the existing order be changed.

Fig. 42: THE TUB. *E. Degas. Louvre, Paris. 1886. 23½″ x 32½″. Pastel—
(Courtesy, Agraci-Art Reference Bureau).*

Fig. 43: JUDGMENT OF PARIS. *A. Renoir. McIlhenny Coll., Philadelphia. c.1914.*
28¾″ x 36¾″—(Courtesy, Henry P. McIlhenny, Philadelphia).

An instance of more moderate change is to be seen in the work of Renoir. THE JUDGMENT OF PARIS, c. 1914, (Fig. 43) is an example of his later preoccupation with figure compositions. The subject is a traditional one, the awarding of the prize to the most beautiful of the goddesses, Venus who had promised Paris the possession of beauty in the person of Helen. Where Impressionism had limited itself to the world revealed by the sense of sight Renoir applied his observations to an ideal image. As an Impressionist, Renoir had explored the appearance of space as filled by light; and that space might be extensive and little defined, as in the MOULIN DE LA GALETTE (Fig. 38). The figures of THE JUDGMENT OF PARIS are bathed in strong sunlight whose power has dissolved the landscape behind them; but they are not lost in the light. Carefully placed along the front plane they present a simple impressive series of masses in relief against the shapelessness of the landscape background. The space that interested Renoir is now a limited and measurable one, that between the figures. Because he has imagined the scene he can adjust his design as he will. He has made the picture not merely reported it. However, after he changed his style, a simple pleasure in the world presented to his senses still pervaded Renoir's work.

There was a more fundamental change among the younger painters. Henri de Toulouse-Lautrec (1864-1901) chose many of the subjects first painted by Degas or Manet; his preference, however, was not for the ballet but for the music hall and for other areas of life even

Fig. 44: CIRCUS FERNANDO. *H. de Toulouse-Lautrec. Art Institute, Chicago. 1888. 38¼″ x 63½″—(Courtesy, The Art Institute of Chicago. The Joseph Winterbotham Collection).*

further out on the fringe of society. The CIRCUS FERNANDO (Fig. 44) makes no pretence of recording observed fact. Everything is painted in summary fashion as if it were of no great matter to record more than the minimum necessary to the design. The casual slice out of the interior of the circus follows the technique of which Degas was master but in a manner which approaches brutality. Only one of the nine or ten persons present is represented whole, the rest being trimmed by the margin. Three are even beheaded in open contempt of the traditional integrity of the human body. It is only the strength and movement of the horse and the demonic control of the ringmaster that Toulouse admired. By exaggerating both the powerful hind quarters of the horse, and the parabolic curve of the ring which sweeps the horse across the canvas and is answered by the

distorted body of the ringmaster he reshaped appearance to give expression to his admiration, in the most vigorous terms.

Toulouse-Lautrec had peculiar physical reasons for his bitterness—he was a dwarf—but others felt equally isolated. For example, Edvard Munch (1863-1944) at the turn of the century constantly repeated themes concerned with the terror of isolation. THE SCREAM (Fig. 45) painted in lurid colours, in themselves as shocking as the scream which the maddened figure utters in the foreground, exposes the indifference of two who approach along a bridge. The landscape, all but empty, has a half-melted, unstable appearance. The broad brush strokes, the strong silhouette lines, and the areas of bright colour serve to flatten the picture. What we see is not the representation of real space but fantasy, a creation of the artist's mind.

44

The maladjustment suggested in the works of Toulouse-Lautrec and Munch had its most striking expression in the career of Vincent Van Gogh (1853-1890): Of educated stock, the son of a Dutch pastor, but from youth by temperament badly equipped to face a world he wished to change, in a short and disastrous career of six years as a painter he left behind him the perfect example of the tragedy of the artist versus society. A short stay in Paris familiarized him with the bright Impressionist palette and permitted him, through a friendship with Gauguin, to enter the inner circle of progressive painters. To Van Gogh light was not only a phenomenon of nature and its heightening of colours a limited artistic problem; rather light was life, and the intensity of colour was the means whereby he could give shape to his intense feeling for life. Following the lead of earlier painters, Monet and Cézanne for instance, he went to the clear atmosphere of Provence. WHEAT FIELD AND CYPRESS TREES, 1889, (Fig. 46) is brilliant beyond the brilliance of the Impressionists. The paint has been so quickly and so vigorously applied that the landscape and the canvas seem to writhe with life. Looking like human beings, the cypresses grow violently upward, while the little flowering trees at the left seem to shrink away from them. Van Gogh always painted in front of the object, as the landscapists of the previous generation had done; but much more came out of him than is to be derived from the evidence presented to his eyes. Even the famous SUNFLOWERS (Fig. 47) of which he painted several versions are animated by a feverish life, expressed in bright yellows, in twisted petals and stalks, and in brushwork that seems to move upon the surface of the canvas.

The harsh energy that can be traced in both the WHEAT FIELD AND CYPRESS TREES and the SUNFLOWERS had its origin in Van Gogh himself, as his numerous self-portraits reveal. In one, (Fig. 11, page 11) he has pictured himself exposed in a glare of light, stripped bare of any glamour, a simple workman-artist. The modelling of the head and body is hard—there is not another portrait in which the skull of the sitter is

Fig. 45: THE SCREAM. *E. Munch. National Gallery, Oslo. 1893. 36" x 29"—(Courtesy, National Gallery, Oslo).*

so obviously felt—and from this head radiate the brush strokes of the background as a wave-like energy released by the head itself. Crammed with this power himself, he saw it everywhere about him. Like Toulouse-Lautrec and Munch, Van Gogh belonged to the new generation of painters who saw the world through their own temperaments.

An alternate course that an artist might take was to search out some spot where the environment was not as hostile. Paul Gauguin (1848-1903) had been a successful banker, then a gifted amateur painter in the company of the Impressionists. When he gave up his business career to become a full-time painter his life became a vivid disclosure of the gulf between the world of the creative artist and the commercial world he had known. Criticism by his relatives and the rapid disappearance of his

Fig. 46: WHEAT FIELD AND CYPRESS TREES. *V. Van Gogh. National Gallery, London. 1889. 28½″ x 25¾″—(Courtesy, The Trustees, The National Gallery of Art, London).*

wealth awoke in him a violent disgust and a romantic hope that he might find a people untouched by the hated European civilization. One remote corner of France, Brittany, was still isolated at the end of the nineteenth century and half mediaeval. THE YELLOW CHRIST (Colour Plate VII) represents a wayside Crucifix, crudely carved, around which peasant women wearing the dress peculiar to their province are kneeling. Behind is a landscape of rounded trees and hills familiar in Brittany, disposed in bands of almost flat colour against which the vertical of the cross stands conspicuously. Around each patch of colour is a separating line corresponding to no phenomenon seen in nature and unused by

artists since the Middle Ages. Having the quality of a line drawn on the canvas it pulls forward each area it encloses to the surface of the painting with the result that the landscape is felt to be both receding and a flat pattern of colours.

Gauguin was not a believer, yet he was deeply moved by the strength and depth of the Bretons' faith that had survived the attacks of modern indifference. He was equally opposed to the conventional taste which in religious art of the time leaned to a sweetened idealism. Hence he chose the pathetically doll-like form of the Christ, painting it yellow to shock the beholder into a greater awareness of the image.

46

Fig. 47: SUNFLOWERS. *V. Van Gogh. Tyson Coll., U.S.A. 1888. 36¼" x 28⅞"—(Courtesy, The Museum of Modern Art. Collection of Carroll S. Tyson Jr.).*

Seeking the more congenial setting of a tropical climate where he could see the exciting colours that he preferred Gauguin went first to southern France, then to Martinique and ultimately to the Marquesas Islands where he died. In the Pacific he came again into contact with a way of life that he felt to be the opposite of Europe's ways. Gauguin was the first to observe the arts of primitive peoples with interest, though he did not confine himself to reproducing those that he discovered in Polynesia; in his work it is possible to find Buddhist and Egyptian borrowings as well. THE DAY OF THE GOD (Fig. 48) is characteristic of his work; the rounded shapes in this symmetrical composition are balanced against a horizontally-banded landscape, the whole effect a summary of the peace he sought. The scheme in which the figures are arranged is entirely artificial and unlike that of the Impressionists of a generation earlier. Incidentally, the two natives at the left exhibit the profile convention of Egyptian art.

The painting reads to the right into depth; this effect is apparent even in black and white, but in colour the recession is more obvious.

Flat areas overlap one another, the more remote being coloured in such a way as to emphasize the recession. Gauguin, like Toulouse-Lautrec and Munch, was attempting to compose simultaneously both in depth and in two dimensions, observing not only the three dimensions of the physical world, but the equally real two dimensions of the painted canvas. This newly challenging artistic problem confronted not only the painters of the last generation of the nineteenth century. The architects felt called upon to show clearly the volume that their buildings contained, the sculptors to stress the solidity of forms in their media, and the painters to take cognizance of the two dimensions of their surfaces. In the next half century the importance of representation in painting continued to diminish and pictorial depth ceased to be measurable. It was about the turn of the century that the reconciliation of represented space and pictorial surface first became an artistic problem.

Most concerned with this problem was Paul Cézanne (1839-1906), once a youthful associate

Fig. 48: THE DAY OF THE GOD. *P. Gauguin. The Art Institute, Chicago. 1894.*
26" x 34½"—(Courtesy, The Art Institute of Chicago. Helen Birch Bartlett
Memorial Collection).

of the Impressionists, but for years withdrawn to his native Aix near Marseille where he painted numerous still lifes and landscapes. Wishing to preserve the brilliant natural colouration of the south of France and at the same time to establish a spatial order, not by the use of perspective or the overlapping of forms, but by the sole device of colour, he painted in patches that recede or advance toward the viewer according to their intensity, tone, size, and relation to adjacent colours. Much of this technique was common knowledge to painters, but never before had this method of ordering form in space been used exclusively. The short, broad brush strokes, rectangular in shape, give a surface pattern to the painting, and at the

same time define his painted volumes as many-faceted surfaces. Cézanne had been struck by the impressive effect of complete orderliness in Poussin's work and wished to emulate it. In a view of MONT STE. VICTOIRE (Colour Plate VIII) the little buildings that dot the slopes are identifiable but have not the quality of solid boxes, let alone, detailed descriptions of dwellings. Trees are feathery, the mountain itself has volume but conveys no suggestion of weight. Everything has place but no substance.

Still lifes offered him even more opportunity to experiment. Easily set up in his studio, long lasting although the fruit is recorded to have rotted as he worked painstakingly over his canvas, they served his purpose well. STILL LIFE

Fig. 49: CARD PLAYERS. *P. Cézanne. Metropolitan Museum, New York. 1890-1892. 25½″ x 32″—(Courtesy, The Metropolitan Museum of Art. Bequest of Stephen C. Clark, 1960).*

(Colour Plate IX) is made up of a few apples, and three pieces of glassware partly buried in a napkin, the whole heaped on a rumpled drape thrown over a table. Objects are depicted with few of the many physical characteristics we know them to have in life. The apples are red and green balls, the drape is so devoid of texture that it is impossible to say of what material it is made. The details that evoke the memory of touch, smell or taste and which were important to the Dutch still life painter of the seventeenth century (See Book II, Fig. 163) are quite neglected. The weight of the fruit or glass is concealed, for nothing has a visible, solid foundation. The still life is hardly more than a colourful composition of plane surfaces, flat, concave and convex.

Exact appearance was of so little concern to Cézanne that the carafe in the centre of the composition bulges to the right, far beyond the symmetry that its model doubtless showed. The distortion has been of the artist's choosing: where he wished to abide by appearance Cézanne could draw a symmetrical vase. That the carafe is not noticeably misshapen at first observation is proof that the spectator feels that balance of the composition is more important than exactness to nature.

Fig. 50: SELF PORTRAIT. *P. Cézanne. Phillips Coll., Washington. 1877. 24" x 18½"—(Courtesy, The Phillips Collection, Washington).*

A similar experimental attitude is to be found in the several versions of the CARD PLAYERS (Fig. 49) that he painted. A group of seated players sometimes accompanied by standing spectators might in the case of another artist have the common activity of the game to unite them; but each man is isolated in his little world by Cézanne, like objects of still life held together by an exact description of their positions within the space created by the painter. The player in the centre, the spectators to the game, the rack of pipes, the drapes were shuffled or removed by Cézanne in the different versions he painted as he searched for a balance of elements. Here they repeat the vertical, horizontal and rounded masses of the three players in front of them. A little off centre to the right they reduce the symmetry of the foreground group; but the

resulting movement of attention to the right is again offset by an attraction into a depth at the left suggested by the darkened wall and diminished scale of the spectator. It is obvious that this kind of composition-game played by Cézanne could go on indefinitely.

This very careful study of forms could hardly be applied to portraiture: the tedium for the sitter would have rendered it intolerable. This may account for the frequency of SELF-PORTRAITS (Fig. 50): he could and did repeatedly paint himself. The paint put on in small square patches of colour gives to his head the appearance of something chiselled from stone. The characteristics of flesh, hair or beard are clearly secondary in importance in his mind to the underlying shape of the head. Rarely, he described himself with some sign of feeling; but usually, as here, there is no sign of emotion. It is as if Cézanne had looked upon himself as another object to be studied.

It is seldom that a Cézanne painting has the appearance of a finished work: each is an experiment laboriously constructed. Because Cézanne's paintings are often of large scale, they form major experiments: consequently, to the generation which followed him Cézanne's work has been a mine of information. He is the great link between the nineteenth- and twentieth-century art of France.

Using a different procedure, Georges Seurat (1859-1891) strove for the pictorial structure that Impressionism had lacked. Much interested in the science of colour, he worked out from his researches a system of light effects much like those of the Impressionists, but so formulated that it dispensed with the need for painting on the spot. Consequently, his SUNDAY AFTERNOON ON THE GRANDE JATTE, (Colour Plate X) an island in the Seine near Paris, is a larger canvas than the Impressionists ordinarily attempted and contains innumerable figures carefully spaced throughout it. Part at least he painted by artificial light following his system. Like his contemporaries he emphasized surface: the dotlike application of paint, called Pointillism, provides the canvas with a tapestry-like texture. Composition in depth is achieved by the repetition

Fig. 51: LA PARADE DE CIRQUE. *G. Seurat. Metropolitan Museum, New York. 1889. 39½″ x 59½″—(Courtesy, The Metropolitan Museum of Art. Bequest of Stephen C. Clark, 1960).*

of similar motifs diminished by distance. Yet there is a careful avoidance of perspective. One does not go back towards a goal; instead, one wanders from point to point. A comparison with Poussin's landscape will reveal the purposelessness of the viewer's movements.

The world that Seurat depicted is a completely rigid one. The human figure is like a piece on a chessboard moved by the designer and without a will of his own. He has no contact with his neighbour, he is not so much an individual as the representative of a type, the labourer, the fashionable lady, or the adolescent girl dreaming over her bouquet. Contrasted with Renoir's MOULIN DE LA GALETTE, SUNDAY AFTERNOON ON THE GRANDE JATTE is a commentary on and not merely the record of people in a crowd. Where the impressionist enjoyed the crowd as life and

change, Seurat depicted isolated beings separated permanently one from the other as so many pegs stuck in the ground.

By the end of his short career Seurat had gone even further towards the destruction of centuries-old conceptions of art. In LA PARADE DE CIRQUE, 1888, (Fig. 51) the figures that appear drawn up in a flat rectangular pattern on the canvas are almost without substance, or individuality. The space they occupy is vague and shallow in depth, and forms are put in it without much attention to a single point of view. We cannot enter into the world of the picture, though like the heads along the bottom of the picture we stand on the edge of it. It was easier for the artist to use the world of entertainment to effect these changes and it is easier for the spectator to accept it.

Fig. 52: THREE MUSICIANS. *P. Picasso. Museum of Modern Art, New York. 1921. 79″ x 87¾″—(Collection, The Museum of Modern Art, New York. Mrs. Simon Guggenheim Fund).*

Fig. 53: Qui Ne Se Grime Pas *(Who Does Not Frown). G. Rouault. Zacks Coll., Toronto. c.1932. 27" x 17½". Aquatint retouched with gouache—(Courtesy, Ayala and Sam Zacks Collection, Toronto).*

Chapter III

PAINTING:

THE TWENTIETH CENTURY

Expressionism

The prophets of modern movements in painting of the twentieth century—Van Gogh, Gauguin and Cézanne—who had painted remote from Paris, and who had died with their work still almost unknown, were given memorial exhibitions in the first six years of the new century. Their art and their example set off a new round of changes. In France a group of painters called by antagonistic critics Les Fauves (The Wild Beasts) wreaked even greater havoc with tradition and the conception of art as the representation of appearance. To an even greater degree, the artists in their paintings tried to record their own excitement; to an even less degree, they troubled themselves about the details of objects. Colours near the limits of intensity were employed in great flat

and emphatic areas in hitherto unused combinations. Pure black was used as a contrast to colour and as a surface calligraphy; and the white underpainting of the canvas was everywhere apparent isolating pure colours so that they would not diminish their strength by optical mixing. The Dance (Fig. 54) by Henri Matisse (1869-1954) painted in 1909, is a pictorial equivalent to the rhythm and pleasure of the dance, expressed as a continuous undulation in a circle. The flowing grace of dancing is made visible in the circlet of joined arms and of contour lines, the latter at once defining both the dancers' movements and the volume of the figures. These contour lines possess flow and beauty and at the same time act as the boundaries of the background spaces that are them-

Fig. 54: THE DANCE. H. Matisse. Walter P. Chrysler Jr. Coll. 1909. 9' x 12'—(Courtesy, The Museum of Modern Art, New York).

selves a part of the pattern. Because THE DANCE is reduced to remarkably few elements, the spectator is clearly and continuously aware of the constant presence of the two-dimensional and three-dimensional aspects of the picture.

Over a long career Matisse continued to paint canvases of high decorative quality in bold, flat areas of colours, strongly two-dimensional and often tapestry-like, the subjects remaining always recognizable even if somewhat modified for the sake of pattern. By his own admission his art was calculated to give pleasure and relaxation; its boldness of colour and its distortions were in harmony with the stimulated modern life we live and were quickly accepted by general taste.

The Fauve landscapes are direct descendants of those of the Impressionists and Gauguin, but brighter and more arbitrary of colour. The extent to which they are landscapes expressing the artist's mood is evident in THREE TREES by Derain, (1880-1954), (Colour Plate XI).

Most Fauvism in France was concerned with pleasurably exciting pictorial values only; but Rouault (1871-1958) used the same bold, simplifying manner to give form to a social and religious message. Trained to work in stained glass, he imparted to his art a mediaeval air. The flat and bright colours are made more violent by the role of black, which takes the place of leading, but is broader and cruder in its application. His choice of themes is a blow to complacency; on the one hand they present the sins of lust or avarice as described in the ugly bodies of those who are the victims of them; on the other they depict the loneliness and sorrow of the abandoned, as in THE CLOWN (Fig. 53). Rouault has been the most important personality in the twentieth-century revival of religious art, the return of which had been prophesied by the lives and spiritual concerns of men like Munch and Van Gogh.

From France the highly-charged painting style of the Fauves spread to Germany where it was to enjoy a longer popularity. There it found a soil already prepared by exhibitions of the art of Van Gogh and Gauguin each of whom had altered appearances the better to display his private feelings. Adopting an even more violent manner than the Fauve group the German painters employed more intense colour, a cruder painting technique and often themes illustrative of extreme brutality. *Expressionism* as it is called in Germany, although the label is equally pertinent to all who used art for the frank portrayal of their own private emotions, remained the affair of organized groups such as Die Brücke (The Bridge) until World War I. In the post-war years it continued to flourish only to be persecuted by the Nazis, who preferred an optimistic idealism embodied in the happy, physically perfect Nordic superman. Not only was Expressionism anarchic in the

Fig. 55: THE LAST SUPPER. E. Nolde. Copenhagen. 1909. 32¼″ x 41¾″—(Courtesy, The Royal Museum of Fine Arts, Copenhagen, Denmark).

eyes of conservatives but several of its practitioners were bitterly critical of modern society and the state. Nolde's THE LAST SUPPER (Fig. 55) is garish in colour, and so fluid in the painting that shapes seem to dissolve. Masks rather than human faces people the canvas: each the over-statement of frenzied excitement. The painting is a private and inverted version of the honoured Christian theme, changed by Nolde to express his contempt for the stiff respectability of conventional religious attitudes and his belief in the need for intense emotion as the basis of religion. The portraits by the German Expressionists are ruthless exposures of anxieties and weaknesses, for the revelation of which only friends and they themselves would sit. Kokoschka's (b. 1886) SELF-PORTRAIT (Fig. 56) in livid unhealthy colours against a sombre ground was painted by one who saw himself as an unhappy person. By contrast Van Gogh's SELF-PORTRAIT (Fig. 11) retains an air of determination in the face of circumstance. West of the Rhine however, expressionist artists rarely saw life as bleakly as did their fellows to the east of it.

Fig. 56: SELF-PORTRAIT. O. Kokoschka. Museum of Modern Art, New York. 1912. 32″ x 19½″—(Collection, The Museum of Modern Art, New York).

Fig. 57: MODERN MIGRATION OF SPIRIT. *C. Orozco.*
Baker Library, Dartmouth College, New Hampshire.
Fresco. 1932-1934. 126″ x 120″—(Courtesy, Dartmouth
College, New Hampshire).

Expressionism broadly based as it was in the art of pre-World War I Europe has played a role ever since, especially when art is called to the support of social criticism or change. It is most clearly visible in Orozco's (1883-1949) art, the Mexican painter of the Revolutionary era. Training in Europe he brought back the Expressionist technique to suggest the primitive powers which contend in a society at war within itself. Distorted bodies, harsh colours, a crowded confusion of space bring back a mediaeval atmosphere like that of the Romanesque in such a painting as MODERN MIGRATION OF THE SPIRIT (Fig. 57). The painting is a twentieth-century equivalent, perhaps, of the Romanesque divine power urging His followers to deeds of conquest at Vézelay.

It became increasingly apparent that the thing represented might be cut to a minimum while the artist could at the same time retain a meaning with power to move the spectator. It was inevitable, and it happened by 1911, that complete abstraction was reached effectively by Wassily Kandinsky (1866-1944), an artist born in Russia but working in Germany. Over a period of three years he gradually simplified, and finally eliminated, the recognizable forms of what previously had been landscapes. The abstractions that resulted were invariably full of movement, both linear and rapid on the one hand, yet like a stain, slowly spreading on the other (Colour Plate XV). They were startlingly bright in colour. To Kandinsky they were statements of his pure feeling, unspoiled by distractions of subject matter, having the quality of music, which is usually quite abstract. It becomes evident, however, that the creator's feelings and the viewer's may not always coincide; and though in time the viewer may learn one artist's language, there is always the difficulty that there are many artists and no common language of pure form. So, though this approach was a logical conclusion to the direction in which art was moving, Kandinsky's kind of abstraction was shelved for a quarter-century.

Cubism

Another kind of abstract art, that making use of geometric figures, is of even earlier date, and had enjoyed many centuries of common use in life and art, but always as symbols of order and the higher powers of men. Like Expressionism, Cubism, as it was called, tended toward complete abstraction, and from its very outset in 1907 was indifferent to the world of appearance. Where Expressionism stressed the feelings of the artist, Cubism was a concentration on the structure of the work of art. The two positions are not mutually exclusive—we find artists who belong in both camps—and they have in common not only a tendency to abstraction, but also a total rejection of the past.

Cézanne had led the way: the apples of his still life, for instance, are coloured balls. Two who followed his lead were Georges Bracque (1882-1963) and Pablo Picasso (1881-........), both working for a time in Paris. The latter, Spanish born, had established himself as an expressionist, his art in successive Blue and Rose periods suggesting first the misery of the poor, THE OLD GUITARIST (Fig. 58) and later the will-of-the-wisp pleasures of memory, as embodied in paintings of actors, acrobats, the circus, and the stage. The colours blue and rose establish the moods, the first more obviously bleak than the gentle warmth of the second. Bracque had been associated with the Fauvists, painting much as the youthful Derain was painting.

THE DEMOISELLES D'AVIGNON, 1907, (Fig. 59) by Picasso is a milestone in Cubism, and even

in modern art. The title means little; indeed, it was attached after the painting was completed. The painting presents a standard academic subject, a group of female nudes posed to form a pictorial unit. But here it becomes a parody of what had been from the Renaissance onwards a concentrated display of the beauty of the female form. The harshness of shapes, the pink and blue colouring, are not particularly new. The novelty lies in the angularity of form, the bodies being planed down to geometric volumes. In the heads of the two figures at the right there is a trace of the new enthusiasm of artists of the time for the art of primitive cultures. West African tribal masks, which were mainly from French colonies, present a similar simplification into flattened geometric volumes (Fig. 206). The unsophisticated brutality of the culture these African images represented, appealed to the young artists, who themselves gloried in the role of young savages. The employment of these primitive arts was slight

Fig. 58: THE OLD GUITARIST. *P. Picasso. Art Institute, Chicago. 1903. 48" x 37⅜"—(Courtesy, The Art Institute of Chicago. Helen Birch Bartlett Memorial Collection).*

Fig. 59: LES DEMOISELLES D'AVIGNON. *P. Picasso.*
Museum of Modern Art, New York. 1907. 96" x 92"—
(Collection, The Museum of Modern Art, New York).

and short-lived. Modern art by its practice of expression through the distorted human body has made primitive art, however, much more interesting in itself.

The subsequent direction of Cubism is towards complete abstraction, until finally only a vestige of form betrays the origin of any particular motif. It is as if the artists wished in their paintings to retain some evidence of their point of departure from ordinary reality by including matter which, after being subjected to an analysis into its many geometric facets, is then seen flat, as is proper to a painting. The flattening process is accompanied by a kind of transparence, the planes seen thereby as layered. If many small pieces of glass are piled atop one

another, an analogous result is obtained, especially when the strata of fragments are not carefully stacked but some penetrate through two or three layers. To simplify their study the early Cubists limited colour to grey and brown drab tones. The artists who painted thus were no longer concerned with the nature of man, PORTRAIT OF VOLLARD (Fig. 60): they were intent on finding how they could combine planes at apparently different distances in space into a non-representational order. The whole previous Western tradition had been to make order out of planes which, at definite distances, had remained constant relative to one another and to the viewer.

A special development from Cubism was the

Fig. 60: PORTRAIT OF VOLLARD.
*P. Picasso. Pushkin Museum,
Moscow. 1910. 36" x 25½"—
(Courtesy, Art Reference Bureau).*

invention of *Collages* which take their name from the French word for glue. Georges Bracque's LE COURRIER, 1913, (Fig. 61) so named by reason of the newspaper headline that is so prominent in its composition is an agglomeration of angular-shaped bits of paper, some painted with wood-graining tools, others removed from newspapers and a cigarette-box wrapper. Mounted on paper and then drawn over, the collage passes from real things like the wrapper to simulated wood and then to the near abstraction of the vague silhouettes of wine glasses and tray. The artist has endeavoured to combine these three levels of existence. The fragments are enough to start a train of images in the observer's mind, and the manner in which the fragments haphazardly overlap corresponds to our knowledge of reality where what is seen is mingled with generalizations of memory based on past observation. The cigarette label and newspaper heading are pieces of an experience which include the simulated grain of the furniture and walls of a café and the even more fundamental shape of glass and tray used in the café. This process is one of assembling where the initial stage of Cubism had been that of taking apart.

The collage is fragile and may deteriorate rapidly into a dusty, faded and limp curiosity. Whereas once a work of art had been carefully made in the prospect of a long period of use, and the artist who had created it was sure that it would be understood for years, the modern painter may take the attitude that the image he has created is necessarily temporary because change is everywhere so rapid. Permanence, he may say, is inconsistent with modern life.

Primitivism

In another way the younger artists of the early twentieth century rejected the cultural heritage of the centuries since the Renaissance. They turned to an extravagant admiration of

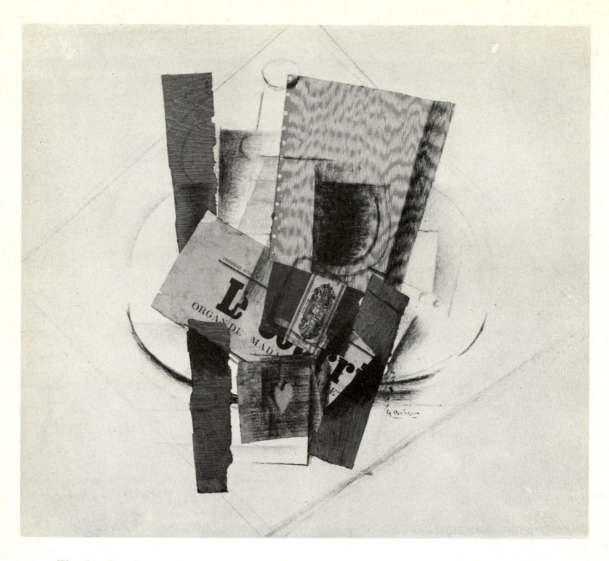

Fig. 61: LE COURRIER. *G. Braque. Philadelphia Museum of Art. 1913. 20" x 22½". Collage—(Courtesy, Philadelphia Museum of Art. A. E. Gallatin Collection).*

the naïve painters, those without formal training yet possessed of a natural ability. Due to the naïve painters' sheer lack of art-school education their canvases were devoid of characteristics which the young artists themselves were discarding: perspective, naturalistic rendering of detail, the simple appearance of things. The naïve or 'primitive' painter is the product of a society that cannot train all its potential artists. In America during the eighteenth and nineteenth centuries all art was a marginal activity of a frontier society. In Europe in the nineteenth and twentieth centuries, aside from the highly trained academic painters supported by the state and a small clientele, there was neither a method of

Fig. 62: THE SLEEPING GYPSY. *Henri Rousseau (le Douanier). Museum of Modern Art, New York. 1897. 51" x 70"—(Collection, The Museum of Modern Art, New York. Gift of Mrs. Simon Guggenheim).*

training nor an outlet for moderate talents in a mechanized industrial society. Henri Rousseau (1844-1910), le Douanier (customs officer) as he is known, was a retired minor government official, a music teacher of sorts, and a painter of portraits as well as of romantic scenes of tropical fairylands. Because the naïve painter is not a self-proclaimed radical, Rousseau's THE SLEEPING GYPSY (Fig. 62) is based on a work by a once famous and now forgotten academic painter of his own day; and its enamel smooth surfaces are like those of conservative painters of a couple of generations earlier. Everything in the picture is crystal clear, lit not by the moonlight but by an unnatural light that has no single source, yet moulds shape and imparts to the scene an air of mystery. Rousseau thought

of each form as a self-contained unit, isolated and distinct, seen in a characteristic position, the lion in profile, the gypsy full face, the mandolin from above, the vase in silhouette. Thus the spatial order no less than the light defies natural laws; but the painting is not confused, for the laws of art are those of the picture and not of the physical world outside the frame.

Talent among naïve painters is a rarity. Rousseau, as an experienced artist of talent in frequent contact with enthusiastic supporters among a younger generation of painters, enjoyed a unique opportunity. He was encouraged, not to be conventional as he would have liked, but to be as fully naïve as possible, to make of this limitation, his personal style.

Futurism

Though some artists had recognized the great changes made in society by the Industrial Revolution and the consequent growth of great cities, none had done more than deplore this change before the Futurists, as they called themselves, came on the scene in the years just before World War I. To them the noise, congestion, speed, and constant change within the city constituted a stimulant to produce paintings with such titles as "The City Rises", or "Dynamism of a Cyclist".

The Futurists took the violence of the night life of Paris to be another sign of the rapid tempo of the time. DYNAMIC HIEROGLYPHIC OF THE BAL TABARIN (Fig. 63) by Severini (b. 1883) is a pictorial description of the shattering glare of artificial light, the syncopated music of the dance hall, the hurried lives of those who went there. In the splinters one can trace such signs as these: a top-hatted man, artificial curls of hair, VALSE, waving flags, bits of lace—the whole in sharply contrasting colour, shoved pell-mell together in space. Movement is suggested by the repetition of curve and angled line, blurred on one edge, as if the same thing were seen twice in rapid succession. It is clear that some of the techniques of Cubism had been given this special meaning by the Futurists.

The inventions of Cubism had suggested already to Fernand Léger (1881-1955) that a composition of semi-mechanical forms of cubes and cylinders could give a symbol for the Machine Age. In THE CITY (Fig. 64) he was later to develop this image of the congestion of the modern metropolis.

Though he paused only momentarily to experiment with the Futurist variant on Cubism, Marcel Duchamp (b. 1887) created in the NUDE DESCENDING A STAIRCASE, No. 2 (Fig. 65) the best-known example of movement pictorially achieved. A human form reduced to plates and discs apparently vibrating is repeated as a series of images in an overlapping sequence so that the flow of time is continuously, if jerkily, me-

Fig. 63: DYNAMIC HIEROGLYPHIC OF THE BAL TABARIN. G. Severini. *Museum of Modern Art, New York. 1912. 63½″ x 61½″ —(Collection, The Museum of Modern Art. Acquired through the Lillie P. Bliss Bequest).*

Fig. 64: THE CITY. *F. Léger. Museum of Art, Philadelphia. 1919. 91″ x 116″—*
(Courtesy, Philadelphia Museum of Art. A. E. Gallatin Collection).

chanical. The emergence of one figure through another is not scientific—two bodies cannot occupy the same space at the same time. What the canvas does is to blend together two separate images, that of the past, or of memory, and that of the present. Thus movement is made visible. Having such an explicit title, the painting seemed, as it was intended to be, a deliberate flouting of the expected: hence the great indignation expressed by spectators who first saw the picture at the Armory Show in New York in 1913.

Dada

When World War I came, the Futurists saw its violence at first as merely the heightening of the tempo of action; but at the end of four years of destruction many artists were prepared to turn their backs on art. To them the world was quite mad and art had no place in it. This is the basis of Dada, an activity partly non-artistic, which took its name from an infant's name for his toy and which aimed to show the silliness of the world and the futility of art in it. Since early in the nineteenth century artists had

Fig. 65: Nude Descending a Staircase, No. 2. *M. Duchamp. Arensberg Coll., Museum of Art, Philadelphia. 1912. 58" x 35"—(Courtesy, Philadelphia Museum of Art. The Louise and Walter Arensberg Collection).*

drifted apart from the mass of men, becoming in the process the more violently convinced of the rightness of their way and of the error of society. For a generation they had taken upon themselves to point out the anarchy into which civilization was falling; but as prophets they had gone unheeded. Dada exhibitions, in which objects including bicycle wheels, snow shovels, and a reproduction of Leonardo's Mona Lisa with a mustache were given elaborate titles, marked the extreme of this protest: at the end of one such show the spectators were provided

with hammers to destroy the exhibits. An indication of the futility felt by this cross-section of the creative world was the abandonment of painting by Marcel Duchamp, who had become the most brilliant of the Dadaists.

The collages of the Dadaists were true trash compositions, put together from the debris of modern civilization. They originate in the collages of a few years earlier.

Dada compositions had often the appearance of haphazardly collected rubbish carefully organized by the artist. Max Ernst, labelled one such work 1 Copper Plate 1 Zinc Plate 1 Rubber Towel 2 Calipers 1 Drainpipe Telescope 1 Roaring Man (Fig. 66) to suggest the meaninglessness of his work and his open rejection of such a small thing as an acceptable title like "Still Life of Modern Objects". The absence of such traditional skills as that embodied in careful brushwork, and the heavy reliance on draughting tools that 1 Copper Plate, etc. shows seem to proclaim that the artist is dead, his place taken by some device as crudely mechanical as the material listed in the contents of the painting.

Synthetic Cubism

After World War I a new start was made to find some basis upon which the artist might build. Picasso restored the human figure to his paintings. The Three Musicians (Fig. 52), consists of three clowns whose metallic angularity and sharp contrasts of colour give visual expression to the strident sounds of modern music. It is built upon the cubist inventions of a decade before and upon the collage. This large canvas is clearly Picasso's attempt to raise cubist painting to a level of importance equal to that of the great figure paintings of the past. Picasso has never since abandoned the human form as the preferred central subject in his canvases. Almost contemporary with The Three Musicians, Mother and Child, (Fig. 67) reflects a simple humanity of the most permanent kind, expressed in heavy slow-moving figures done in plain earth colours against a neutral ground. It can be compared with the sculpture

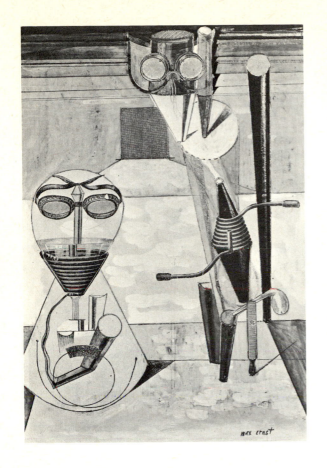

Fig. 66: 1 Copper Plate, 1 Zinc Plate, 1 Rubber Towel, 2 Calipers, 1 Drainpipe Telescope, 1 Roaring Man. *M. Ernst. Coll. Hans Arp. 1920. 12" x 9". Collage —(Courtesy, The Museum of Modern Art. Collection, Hans Arp, Meudon, France).*

Fig. 67: Mother and Child. *P. Picasso. Art Institute, Chicago. 1921. 56¼" x 64"—(Courtesy, The Art Institute of Chicago).*

Fig. 68: COMPOSITION No. 2. P. Mondrian. Guggenheim Museum, New York. 1922. 21¾" x 21"—(Courtesy, The Solomon R. Guggenheim Museum).

of Maillol who also strove after a kind of peasant classicism to suggest the ancient and continuing values of mankind.

The Dutch painter Mondrian (1872-1944), who had begun his studies before World War I, worked patiently to discover in simple rectangular units the balances of shape and colour that would produce the satisfaction of orderly relation (Composition No. 2, Fig. 68). It should be emphasized, however, that there is no precise arithmetical ratio between areas of colour in his paintings. The relation still depends on the highly personal judgment of the artist. Nevertheless, Mondrian's studies in asymmetrical compositions have been immensely useful to architectural designers, the makers of posters, and printers. He has done more than any other man to destroy the ancient passion for symmetry, for his canvases have demonstrated so many alternatives to symmetry that art has been much enriched by his studies.

In the final years of his life Mondrian increased the size of his canvases, reduced the scale of his units and softened the hitherto rigid structure of rectangular bars that he had used for years. These last became two-toned sequences weaving through the larger areas of colour. The title given BROADWAY BOOGIE WOOGIE (Fig. 69) expresses the greater excite-

ment of the pattern when in place of the careful weighing of the relations of a few parts the eye is moved abruptly and at an irregular pace back and forth. With the black grid removed, moreover, the colours are released from the surface of the canvas to appear as if they were located in depth, the depth depending on the colour and size of adjacent areas.

Another line of attack has been to try to retrieve the sheer innocence of man before the rise, duration, and fall of the tradition that had perished with Dada, the death of art. Paul Klee (1879-1940), through a careful study of child art, as well as that of the most primitive cultures, arrived at something like the art of a very wise child, THE TWITTERING MACHINE (Fig. 70). Like the child's, his art is of the mind's eye, is economical in its use of all unnecessary accessories, and is entirely two-dimensional; but unlike the child's, it is not marred by uncertainties, is very subtle in technique and colour, is carefully related to the available paper or canvas space, and either in the painting itself or in the title that it bears, there is always an adult's sophistication. Klee's paintings constitute the 'Alice in Wonderlands' of the twentieth century, having the same appeal to adults as that storybook.

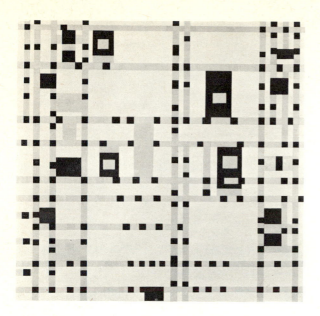

Fig. 69: BROADWAY BOOGIE
WOOGIE. *P. Mondrian. Museum of
Modern Art, New York. 1943. 50″
x 50″—(Collection, The Museum of
Modern Art, New York).*

Fig. 70: THE TWITTERING MACHINE.
*P. Klee. Museum of Modern Art,
New York. 1922. 16½″ x 12″.
Watercolour and ink—(Collection,
The Museum of Modern Art, New
York).*

Fig. 71: I AND THE VILLAGE.
*M. Chagall. Museum of Modern
Art, New York. 1911. 7⅝″ x 59½″
—(Collection, The Museum of
Modern Art, New York. Mrs. Simon
Guggenheim Fund).*

Surrealism

Other painters have resorted to the fantasies of dreams or memory images. Coming as they do from an interior source they are not spoiled by contact with the world of everyday experience, the values of which many artists have come to despise. Marc Chagall (b. 1877), who grew up as a Jewish lad in a remote Russian town, had memories of childhood that swam vaguely about in his consciousness. The many facets of these memories he blended together on his canvas. The drawing is deliberately naïve and childlike, the colours gay. Both Klee and Chagall arrived at their ultimate way of painting through the most advanced "isms" of the century, Klee in German Expressionism, Chagall through Cubism. The transparent planes of Chagall's I AND THE VILLAGE (Fig. 71) bear witness to this. His fantasies are invariably happy ones.

Fig. 72: MELANCHOLY AND THE MYSTERY OF
THE STREET. *G. di Chirico. Private Coll.,
Connecticut. 33½″ x 27¼″—(Courtesy, The
Museum of Modern Art, New York. Collec-
tion, Mr. and Mrs. Stanley S. Resor).*

Fig. 73: COMPOSITION. *J. Miro. Wadsworth Atheneum, Hartford, Connecticut. 1933. 51″ x 63½″—(Courtesy, The Wadsworth Atheneum, Hartford).*

More threatening are the paintings by Giorgio di Chirico (b. 1888). These portray unending perspectives, menacing shadows, and strange juxtapositions of familiar objects in a disturbing landscape just a little out of perspective, MELANCHOLY AND THE MYSTERY OF THE STREET (Fig. 72). Other artists reveal the shapes of even more formless obsessions in amoeba-like shapes adrift in a dimensionless ground that has colour and a quality of depth. Joan Miro's COMPOSITION (Fig. 73) exposes a fantasy in which emerging and dissolving blobs swim aimlessly about, becoming opaque or fading into an outline. The painter has permitted himself a complete release from all the controls imposed by what lies outside himself. What has come out of him seems harmless enough: some other artists trace more violent forms.

In the 1920's the Surrealist painters, as they termed themselves, tried to discover an automatic system of recording whatever came by chance into their minds. Chance in this case was not accident, but a coming to the surface of images from the lower levels of being. The understanding of these revelations of the subconscious has been aided by modern psychoanalysis; moreover, the interest of artists in the exposure of their innermost desires reflects the widespread attention given to the subconscious in a large part of our culture. Yet it is impossible to dispense with careful thought or to wipe out the experience that an artist accumulates in his training. Between the consciousness of the fantasy and its record, there is always some old-fashioned artistry. Surrealism and fantasy in art are not very much different from the effects produced by the paintings of Kandinsky in the first decade of the century or by Munch at the end of the nineteenth. The recognizability of the images has decreased making the viewer's role more difficult at the same time as the artist's self-examination has become more searching.

Fig. 74: GUERNICA. *P. Picasso. Museum of Modern Art, New York. 1937. 11'6"*
x 25'8"—(On extended loan to The Museum of Modern Art, New York, from the
artist, P. Picasso).

The 1930's and the years that immediately succeeded World War II were times of general social concern. The artists ranged themselves so firmly on the side of humanity and justice, that the complete futility which characterized the crisis of World War I did not appear. The human figure could assume an important role in art; it was at this time, that the sculptor, Henry Moore (b. 1898), matured; it was at this time also that Picasso created perhaps his best-known painting, GUERNICA (Fig. 74), in 1937. A large canvas 12 by 26 feet, painted for the Spanish pavilion in the Paris exhibition of that year, it commemorates the destruction of the Spanish city of Guernica by German dive bombers. The fragmented shapes, angular and flat, that overlap one another are the familiar materials of cubism, the exaggeration of human and animal forms being in the tradition of Expressionist distortion. But modern though it is, Guernica appeals strongly as well to those with a sense of the continuity of history. Compositionally speaking, there is in the centre a great triangular disposition of forms flanked by two rectangular areas, one at each side, both containing variations on the theme presented in the central triangle. It is a Renaissance composition, pyramidal in structure, adapted to modern use; and the sense that we are looking at an old convention raises the Guernica to something of more permanent importance than the recording of an event dated 1937, painted in a contemporary style.

The fracturing of appearance in Cubism had started as an artistic analysis; it had been used by Picasso in the THREE MUSICIANS as a development of Expressionism; but in Guernica it is used not only to convey the artist's horror at the spiritual and moral chaos which prompted the obliteration-bombing on that occasion, but also to portray the literal, physical destruction of the city. Much of the painting is easily read and immediately acceptable. Guernica is painted in black, white and grey, the bleak colours of a grim message, the tones of night and the signs of the spiritual darkness of the dead. Some of the forms are private symbols introduced by Picasso, for example, the triumphant bull and

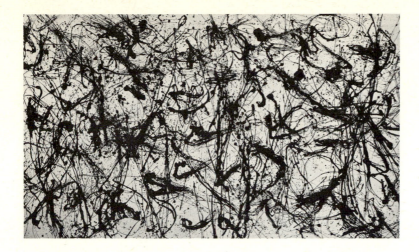

Fig. 75: NUMBER 32. *Jackson Pollock. Private Coll., U.S.A. 1950. 9' x 15'1"—(Courtesy, Marlborough-Gerson Gallery, Inc. New York).*

the screaming horse. Derived from the Spanish bull ring, the bull is the image of bestial strength, here presented as the destroyer of the weaker horse, who stands for the defenseless citizens of Guernica.

The glaring electric light contrasted with the feeble oil lamp is more difficult to explain; but even here the constantly reappearing role of light symbolism in the history of art opens possibilities of investigation. The great modern work of art, be it literary, musical, pictorial, or sculptured, is to the creator an exploration into the furthest recesses of his conscious and subconscious self; it is, however, an infinitely more uncertain voyage for those who follow where he has led.

In the 1950's artists again turned away from the human image. Save for the veterans, headed by Picasso, who remain from the extraordinarily varied and fruitful first third of the century, the painters who came to maturity in the 1940's and 1950's turned again to abstractionism, many painting in forms indicative of violent energy. Called Action Painting, the new trend was a close linking of the making of the painting as physical act with the creative impulse which directs it. Ideally, an Action painter, such as Jackson Pollock (1912-1956) NUMBER 32 (Fig. 75) surrendered himself, allowing whatever impulses stir him to direct his attack on the canvas. A refinement of the wish to eliminate what is

premeditated from his performance, this trend is only a variant on earlier efforts made by the Surrealists. The paint may be brushed on; but it may also be trowelled, thrown, or allowed to drip upon the canvas. The last two procedures point to a new element in painting—deliberately courted chance or accident; but the splash of paint becomes then a challenge and a stimulus around which the painter weaves his reactions in the form of painted abstract forms. The psychologists had already used the blot technique to search the subconscious since the 1930's. Another peculiarity of the 1950's has been the immensity of the canvases; in the eyes of the painter this immensity has offered a greater physical challenge and the exhilaration of a major conquest when completed.

The long rule of Paris had been broken by World War II, and it was in the United States that this major Abstractionist tendency had its beginnings. It has, however, become a worldwide manifestation, being readily communicable because it has no traditional roots to cause misunderstandings between cultures. It is, accordingly, acceptable to a world that is coming slowly to recognize that whereas the art of the past is a storehouse of the achievements that reveal man's diverse possibilities, the work of the living painter is concerned with the revelation of his present position in a world community of increasing uniformity.

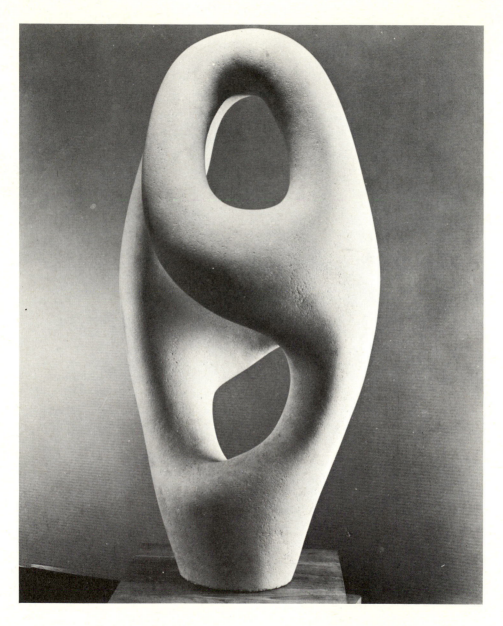

Fig. 76: PTOLEMY. *H. Arp. Private Coll., New York.*
1953. 40½″ high. Limestone—(Courtesy, The Hon-
orable and Mrs. Wm. A. M. Burden, New York).

Fig. 77: DANCER LOOKING AT THE SOLE OF HER FOOT. *E. Degas. 1882-1895. 18" high. Bronze—(Courtesy, The Metropolitan Museum of Art, New York).*

Chapter IV

MODERN MOVEMENTS IN SCULPTURE

Painting was the leading art during the nineteenth century: generation followed generation of artists whose reputations have survived the complete change of standards of the twentieth century. It was, however, a dark age for sculpture. At its beginning, sculptors were blinded by the general admiration of an antiquity they knew only through second-rate Roman copies wherein a process of simplification, common to copies, had been misinterpreted as idealization of the human figure. The near absence of ancient paintings had protected painters against a similar misunderstanding. Their transposition of sculptured forms into two dimensions had given painters at least a measure of freedom and the line drawing on Greek vases might modify but could not control the nature of oil painting. Sculpture remained clamped in

formulas calling for classical subjects cut in marble—the men presented as noble athletes, the women as graceful nymphs.

Only the portrait escaped, for a time, this dullness. The busts of the Frenchman Houdon (1741-1828) combined a care for exact physical details—he made plaster masks of his sitters—with a forceful expression of the most characteristic public aspect of personality. It was an age in which individuals were at their best in playing public roles, and the world saw events of the time as the actions of great men. It was, for example, Wellington who beat Napoleon at Waterloo, not a coalition of Europe re-establishing the balance of power. Houdon has provided history with the busts of such men as Voltaire, Franklin, Washington and Napoleon. Unlike the Baroque portrait in which the motion of the

Fig. 78: WASHINGTON. *J. A. Houdon. State Capitol, Richmond, Virginia. 1788-1792. 74″ high. Marble—(Courtesy, Virginia Chamber of Commerce).*

Can one even momentarily imagine a sculptured equivalent to a sun-soaked Monet landscape? The sculptor was left to keep company with those who opposed the modern movements.

There was no lack of demand for sculpture; yet it was generally an unhealthy patronage, too often given by public bodies relying upon committee judgments. The choices were usually no more than a compromise. As the century went on, the demand produced some deplorable working practices. The sculptor was forced to rely too much on assistants for the execution of his ideas, often carried no further than a small plaster model that had to be expanded to its final size by a method of mechanical measurement. What the master created, his helpers had to transfer to much larger surfaces, and in the process the work lost all subtlety. Original intention and final result became widely separated. It is very rare to see, adorning a public monument, a piece of nineteenth-century sculpture that is not coarse and monotonous in execution.

THE DEPARTURE OF VOLUNTEERS IN 1792 (Fig. 79) or the *Marseillaise* by François Rude (1784-1855) is almost the only sculpture decorating architecture that has been able to surmount these obstacles. The subject was one capable of rousing the feelings of patriotic Frenchmen, Rude among them, who could recall the glories of the previous generation and romantically contrast them with the dull Second Republic under which they were living. The dress may be Roman and the allegory of Victory antique, but the profusion of weapons, the violence of gesture, and diagonals of the composition are the inheritance of another age, the Baroque, when grand themes like this relief were constantly employed. Rude's contemporary, the painter Delacroix, was equally indebted to the seventeenth century. Seen close at hand, the work is cluttered with detail and hard in execution but the relief was made to be observed at a distance, scaled against the side of the immense arch. Then, edges become blurred and soft, and the animation appears more real by contrast with the inert mass and smooth surface of the monument.

head, the shoulders and even the dress adds to understanding, Houdon's portraits are simply heads. In this, they follow the Roman practice of Republican and early Imperial times, an imitation appreciated by Houdon's contemporaries as the highest form of flattery. For instance, his portrait of WASHINGTON (Fig. 78), with large head held erect on a massive neck, eyes big-socketed, nose coarse, mouth set in a tight horizontal line, jaw outthrust, and glance up-raised, embodies steadfastness even in adversity, the ideal of conduct in a Roman statesman. Like portrait painting, portrait sculpture had no future in the nineteenth century.

Neo-classicism was only the initial handicap, however; the trend of painting towards an ever greater dependence on simple vision and on the whole physical environment as the theme of art mirrored an interest unsatisfied by sculpture.

Fig. 79: DEPARTURE OF THE VOLUN-
TEERS. *F. Rude. Arc de Triomphe,
Paris. 1833-1836. c.42' x 26'—(Cour-
tesy, Archives Photographiques).*

The nineteenth century saw the beginning of the painter turned temporarily sculptor. Painters, who habitually employed the human figure, modelled to test themselves in a medium so backward that it offered no work by contemporary sculptors to serve as a basis for comparison. Géricault, Daumier, Degas, Renoir, and Gauguin all experimented, and save for Gauguin did not publicly exhibit their findings. Degas is best known for his dancers and horses. Based on innumerable drawn and painted studies, his sculptures reveal a knowledge of form poised or in action. An example, DANCER LOOKING AT THE SOLE OF HER FOOT (Fig. 77) has caught a moment of equilibrium in which the whole body takes part to make possible the balance. Degas' understanding of the possibilities of a three-dimensional medium like sculpture prompted him to choose a pose in which the limbs reach forward and back, up and down from the torso to make use of all the dimensions of this art. This generally unknown work, often of very high quality, seems to indicate that the art of painting drew away several who would have made names as sculptors in other times.

The single important professional sculptor of the century was the French artist, Auguste Rodin (1840-1917) rightly regarded as the first of modern sculptors. It was he who introduced several new conceptions into sculpture, for example, the fragment of the body as a complete work of art, the form emerging from the block of marble from which it has been carved, or the bronze showing the distinctive marks of the clay model from which it was made. It will be noticed that none of these innovations conformed either to antique practice or to observation from life. To Rodin, the human body was the voice of the human soul torn by such passions as love, fear, anger, or despair. The *Gates of Hell,* his greatest commission, was intended to be the doors of a school of applied design that was never built. This effort of the scope of the Gothic portals or of Michelangelo's Sistine chapel frescoes was to express Rodin's beliefs about man. The doors themselves were never completed; but numerous groups and single figures taken from them were cast or carved, the best known of which is THE THINKER (Fig. 80). In the original scheme, this was placed above the centre of the doors and

75

Fig. 80: THE THINKER. *A. Rodin. Metropolitan Museum, New York. 1889. 27½″ high. Bronze—(Courtesy, The Metropolitan Museum of Art. Gift of Thomas F. Ryan, 1910).*

however, the thoughts that stir them are related to a higher power, the Hebraic Creator of the world and man, or the Christian Judge of mankind. In the late nineteenth century, traditional religious solutions were called in doubt and it was easier to feel the weight of man's problems than find an answer to them. The body of Rodin's figure is simply blocked out, its volumes defined further by the strongly tactile surface, corrugated by the knots and angles of muscle and bone. Furthermore, the body bearing evidence of the final applications of clay brings closer to the viewer the creator whose handiwork is literally traceable in these dabs. Compared to it, the polished marbles and bronzes of earlier sculptors seem very impersonal. The two major claims Rodin made for sculpture, namely, that it should display the artist's inner feelings and that it should vigorously assert its three-dimensional nature, have been the basis of all later sculptors' work. Only by their departure from the human body as the sole language of their art and in their exploration of the problem of space have they gone markedly beyond him.

A second commission was a memorial to Balzac (Fig. 81) the great French novelist. Wishing to escape from the conventional statue of the nineteenth century which seemed hardly more than a physical likeness perched atop bronze clothing, Rodin aimed to bring out the great power and mystery of the creative artist in a hulking mass of cloak-wrapped body culminating in a head whose semblance to Balzac was more spiritual than physical. The mass is roughly finished to suggest an unrefined and primitive strength, and set a little off the vertical to overcome the effect of inert stability. Rodin himself had trouble enough discovering sculptural means to convey his notion of the writer: the public were quite incapable of following him. The commission was never completed.

A couple of generations later Rodin's energetic interpretation of form became so accepted, however, that a follower of his, Jacob Epstein (1880-1960), was a hugely successful portrait sculptor. His bust of George Bernard Shaw (Fig. 82) exhibits the aggressiveness of the

looked down upon the evidences of the hell of man's own making—the consuming fires of his own passions. With the realization of man's predicament, THE THINKER tenses instinctively. The physical power of the body is alive in the tense muscles of the lower legs and the braced feet, but it diminishes throughout the rest of the body to the point where the power of the mind has rendered the left arm quite limp and has turned the right into a great prop to hold the heavy head. Before the puzzle of man's purpose, THE THINKER is rendered powerless. THE THINKER's pose is one long familiar in art. There is one like it, but more frontal, in Michelangelo's LAST JUDGMENT fresco (see Book II, Fig. 48); another in the person of Jeremiah on the ceiling of the Sistine Chapel by the Renaissance master (See Book II, Fig. 51). In both cases,

Fig. 81: BALZAC. *A. Rodin. Musée Rodin, Paris. 1892-1897. 9'10" high. Plaster — Courtesy, Bulloz-Art Reference Bureau).*

Rodin, the sculptor, is an isolated figure in the late nineteenth century, but painters were heading in the same direction. Some, like Van Gogh and Munch, discerning the same destructive tendencies in the modern world, modified what they saw, the better to describe how they felt. In addition, many painters of the day, by insisting on the two-dimensionality of painting, took the same stand as Rodin for the three-dimensionality of his medium, sculpture.

Fig. 82: GEORGE BERNARD SHAW. *J. Epstein. National Gallery of Canada, Ottawa. 1934. 16½" high. Bronze—(Courtesy, The National Gallery of Canada, Ottawa).*

writer in its corrugated surface and bristling contours. The energy so exhibited now seemed a positive gain to character once the idea of a simple physical record of appearance was abandoned. The Renaissance or Baroque sculptor had a commonly accepted language of interpretation: a king could look as commanding as his office demanded and still retain his recognizable appearance. A nineteenth century sculptor was faced with the definition of someone more complicated, the creative genius, isolated, heroic and tortured by the strain of his genius.

Fig. 83: THE MEDITERRANEAN. A. Maillol. Museum of Modern Art, New York. c.1901. 41" high. Bronze—(Collection, The Museum of Modern Art, New York. Gift of Stephen C. Clark).

The first of the twentieth-century sculptors was Aristide Maillol (1861-1944). Emphasizing the bulk of forms, he too made clear this long-neglected aspect of sculpture. THE MEDITERRANEAN (Fig. 83) is characteristic of the use of the nude figure in twentieth-century terms in that the anatomy has been simplified into forms approaching the regularity of geometry. The spectator is very much aware of them as separate parts, as, for example, the right arm or the right thigh. Later sculptors carried the process further. The massive proportions and contained contours of the statue make for a very compact form, the embodiment of a serenity just the opposite of THE THINKER. Without in any sense being a copyist, Maillol has struck a note similar to that of Greek sculptors of the fifth century B.C. By calling the seated woman THE MEDITERRANEAN, Maillol has asserted the enduring value of the classical tradition born in the Mediterranean basin. In place of the tension between body and spirit, there is an entire harmony of the two.

An almost opposite attitude was assumed by Wilhelm Lehmbruck (1881-1911), a German sculptor for a time resident in Paris, where he was a pupil of Rodin. In his KNEELING WOMAN (Fig. 84) there is also simplification, but towards very thin forms angularly put together. Since

Fig. 84: KNEELING WOMAN. W. Lehmbruck. Museum of Modern Art, New York. 1911. 69½" high —(Collection, The Museum of Modern Art, New York. Abby Aldrich Rockefeller Fund).

Fig. 85: MAN DRAWING A SWORD. *E. Barlach. Cranbrook Academy of Art, U.S.A. 1911. 29½". Oak— (Courtesy, Galleries-Cranbrook Academy of Art. Bloomfield Hills, Michigan).*

silhouette, rather than volume, is emphasized and the bodily proportions are elongated, the KNEELING WOMAN has a vaguely mediaeval air. This wraithlike body gives form to the deep melancholy of the sculptor, who ended his own life by suicide.

A third sculptor, Ernst Barlach (1870-1938), like Lehmbruck and German artists generally of the first third of the century was troubled by the grossly material nature of contemporary Europe. Engraver and playwright, he was one of several who found in the lower peasants' stunted but powerful bodies, adapted by hardship to existence and guided by instinct rather than a condemnation of the forces that brutalized them, a tribute to man's endurance and the proof of indestructible energies. MAN DRAWING A SWORD (Fig. 85) is made of oak, a tough material the roughly-finished surface of which still bears the mark of the chisel proclaiming the work of the carver. The facets of the sculpture are large and few, the gestures simple and full, the act that of one who fights to live. Barlach's sculptures have many mediaeval reminiscences,

the wood for instance, and the oneness of garment and body. Several of his works have been placed in the settings of mediaeval churches.

The twentieth-century sculptor has constantly turned to the art of earlier periods, neglecting only the portion that begins with the Renaissance and goes down to the nineteenth century. Such borrowing has not resulted in outright imitation but has served rather to widen the range of possibilities within the medium. The sculptures of distant, primitive, and ancient peoples have yielded most new suggestions of forms. Perhaps the keenest interest was that shown in African sculpture, in the decade before World War I. Besides playing a role in Cubist painting, it also gave the first glimpse of a kind of sculpture at the opposite pole to anything then known in the European tradition. The part played by these external stimuli has been rapidly diminishing in the last twenty years as contemporary sculpture finds its directions in its own immediate environment.

Fig. 86: HEAD OF A WOMAN. *P. Picasso. The Art Gallery of Ontario, Toronto. 1909. 21½″ high. Bronze—(Collection, The Art Gallery of Ontario, Toronto. Purchase 1949).*

Picasso who from time to time has turned sculptor improvised his HEAD OF A WOMAN (Fig. 86), a form composed of disintegrating segments of the oval of the head. The object has been to reorder these fragments, balancing those which have been slipped forward against those that recede to form areas of light and shadow. These segmental masses circling as they do around the core, produce a constant effect of unstable movement in the head. So in his painted portraits of the time (Fig. 60), traces of humanity remain beneath this shattered surface, but they are vestiges only of a tradition of representation not easily abandoned even when the intent of the artist has turned to the quite different purpose of a non-representational order.

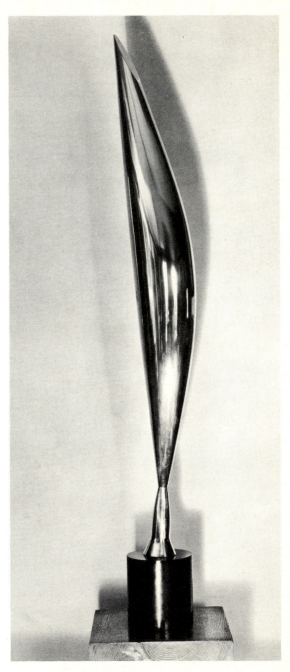

Fig. 87: BIRD IN SPACE. *C. Brancusi. Museum of Art. Philadelphia. 1925. 54″ high. Bronze on marble base—(Courtesy, Philadelphia Museum of Art. The Louise and Walter Arensberg Collection).*

Fig. 88: Sculpture for the Blind. *C. Brancusi. Museum of Art, Philadelphia. 1924. 12" x 6". Marble—(Courtesy, Philadelphia Museum of Art. The Louise and Walter Arensberg Collection).*

The first to detach himself completely from the past was the Roumanian-born resident of Paris, Constantin Brancusi (1876-1957). Like Picasso, Brancusi used the strange and the near abstract forms of African carvings to serve as a bridge to new conceptions. His polished bronze Bird in Space, (Fig. 87) 1925, was only the most famous of a series of works of a like character he had been doing since about 1910. The form seems to turn on its point, moving counter clockwise as well as describing an arc upwards. Streaks of light, flashing up its smooth surface, link movement and light together and this becomes a prolonged and varying effect in time as one walks around the Bird. Birds, as traditionally represented, had been static images based on a compilation of observations and even when apparently flying, they remained frozen in time and place. By laying the whole stress on flight, Brancusi has struck a very modern note, and one which painters, particularly the Futurists, have also sounded.

The Bird in Space is not the first example of sculpture that develops as we walk around it, but what generally resulted in earlier times was a series of separate impressions, not a continuous one. To obtain the same effect, sculpture has also been put on a turntable or set to turn idly in the wind. The base upon which the Bird in Space is set is also of Brancusi's making. This and other pedestals are superimpositions of simple geometric shapes, as important in the sculptor's eyes as the object atop them, the whole becoming a kind of primitive totem. Finally, it will be noted that the surface of the base and that of the Bird are very different, the one slippery smooth and therefore particularly suitable to swift movement, the other rough and strongly suggestive of the weight of stone. This kind of appeal is to be found in certain of Brancusi's egglike forms termed Sculptures for the Blind (Fig. 88). They are to be understood as held objects, whose weight, shape and texture a blind man might appreciate. Brancusi was the first to claim openly that a knowledge of sculpture is not gained solely through the vision but is also dependent on touch, and the perception of weight which, after childhood, we take in remotely through the eyes. By varying textures and the use of materials of known different weights, the modern sculptor has emphasized the sensory channels through which he can communicate with his audience.

Fig. 89: THE GREAT HORSE. *R. Duchamp-Villon. The Art Institute, Chicago. 1914. 17″ high. Bronze—(Courtesy, The Art Institute of Chicago. Gift of Miss Margaret Fisher).*

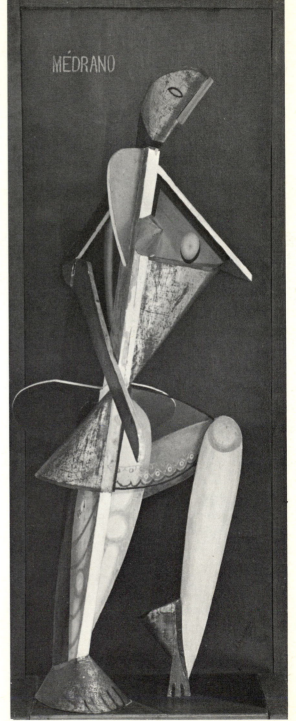

Fig. 90: MEDRANO. *A. Archipenko. Guggenheim Museum, New York. 1915. 50″ high. Wood, tin, oil-cloth, etc.—(Courtesy, The Solomon R. Guggenheim Museum).*

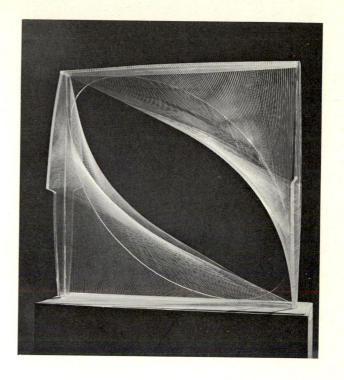

Fig. 91: CONSTRUCTION. *Naum Gabo. Phillips Coll., Washington. 1943. 24¼" high. Lucite—(Courtesy, The Phillips Collection, Washington).*

One stage more abstract is Raymond Duchamp-Villon's (1876-1918) GREAT HORSE (Fig. 89), wherein the forms are reminiscent of the springs, rods and cylinders of a machine in action, a twentieth-century equivalent of the power of the horse. Retaining a more representative appearance are the sculptures of Archipenko assembled from geometrically shaped units. His robot figure, MEDRANO, (Fig. 90) is made of the materials of modern life, wood, tin and oil-cloth, and is formed to suggest regular machine-shaped contours and surfaces. In the second decade of the century, both Duchamp and Archipenko shared with painters like Leger a conviction that mechanization was the supreme moulding influence on modern life.

It was a short step from this point to pure abstraction in the work of a whole generation of Russian sculptors whose appearance coincided with the Russian revolution. The sculptures of Antoine Pevsner (1886-......) and Naum Gabo (1890-......) bear a striking resemblance to the more elaborate models used in solid geometry. The form is defined now as volume, now as *two-dimensional* sheets of glass or plastic and in colour, adding visual complications to the relations of planes as one sheet is seen through another (Fig. 91). Transparency provides many new distance relationships but it may obliterate volume and mass. In Gabo's work particularly, sculpture becomes almost lines in space, weaving in and out as thin bands of material, or as the less translucent edges of glass or plastic. The placing of these constructions on a pedestal is for the purpose of display. Apparently they need no support for they have no appearance of weight.

Fig. 92: LOBSTER TRAP AND FISH TAIL. *A. Calder. Museum of Modern Art, New York. 1939. Approx. 9'6" long. Steel wire and sheet aluminum—(Collection, The Museum of Modern Art, New York).*

Some sculptors have attempted to sever connection with the ground by suspending their creations in air, where, freed of the earth, there is the possibility of composing forms moving in space. The best known of the MOBILES, (Fig. 92) as they are called, are by the American Calder. Two-dimensional sheets, joined by wires serving as the visible reminders of the rhythmical relations of the plates, are hung in a careful balance. The designer has openly become co-partner with natural laws, and, when a slight breeze stirs the mobile moving the creation about in space and forming new relations of its various parts, it is apparent that the artist is playing with chance in an attempt to give shape to patterns not yet clearly foreseeable. This new role of the sculptor can be matched in contemporary painting. Where once an artist felt himself possessed of a thorough grasp of an idea, a modern creator may rely on much outside his power to control.

Not all artists are prepared to go this far. However natural mobiles are in an age in which great patterns of spatial movement are everywhere apparent, they make too complete a surrender of many of the traditional uses of sculpture, and in so doing have not supplanted the earthbound, and even human, form. The English sculptor Henry Moore (b. 1898) has habitually used shapes whose humanity is primordial (Fig. 93). Some, to peer dimly about, raise their heads from the earth to which their bodies seem rooted; others having tiny skulls perched on massive bodies seem motivated more by their instinct than by their reason. Like the rough stone or great logs out of which he has carved them, his figures seem moulded by natural forces. A comparison with Michelangelo's CREATION OF MAN on the Sistine ceiling (see Book II, Fig. 49) must lead the observer to conclude that a twentieth-century artist is no longer hopeful of the perfection of man but merely of his power to survive, and even survival is on the simplest terms.

Moore has consistently found his imagery in man as the titles of his works declare—*Mother and Child, Family Group, Women Talking, Seated King and Queen, Falling Warrior.* To reach this position, he has moved away from a more abstract youthful style. The same is true of Jacques Lipchitz (b. 1891) who at the outset was much indebted to African sculpture but has grown to prefer mythological and religious themes in which, by an act of violence, man holds off the forces against him. PROMETHEUS STRANGLING THE VULTURE (Fig. 94) recalls man's ability to resist successfully the cruelties of tyrants. Where Moore indicated endurance, Lipchitz illustrates striving. Both sculptors ensure the human response to their works by stressing weight; but, where Moore's group lies on the ground, Lipchitz' group is hazardously entrusted to the balance of a point. The weathered stone of one and the rapidly applied lumps of clay of the other mark in the materials themselves the difference between themes and sculptors. In both cases, the element

of representation is severely reduced. Lipchitz diminishes it to a greater degree than Moore because he wishes to suggest the turbulence and intermingled confusion of the struggle. Arms, legs, wings and bodies are almost indistinguishable and possibly even unnaturally duplicated as Lipchitz passes beyond illustration to the heroic violence at the heart of the myth. Both sculptors pierce their solids with holes, Moore particularly, though he is not the inventor of this device. Although the holes can be used to further the suggestion of the attrition of time, they are also passages through which the spectator's consideration of any one aspect is led towards an aspect otherwise not revealed. The awareness of volume and shape is increased in the process of exploration.

Fig. 93: RECLINING FIGURE. *H. Moore. Tate Gallery, London, England. 1938. c.54" long. Stone—(Courtesy, The Tate Gallery, London).*

85

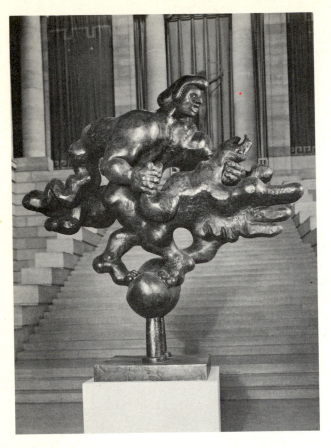

Fig. 94: PROMETHEUS STRANGLING THE VULTURE. *J. Lipchitz. Museum of Art, Philadelphia. 1949. 7'9" x 7'8" including base. Bronze — (Courtesy, Philadelphia Museum of Art).*

The invitation to explore can be particularly felt in the sculpture of Hans Arp (Fig. 76), the inventor of the device of holing. Here, the absence of human representation allows one to see, without distractions, the formal processes. By the passage of the hole, any one view of the sculpture encourages to an observation of what is hinted at through the aperture; and that hint leads on to something else. Just as the sculptor has increased the appeal of sculpture by making much of its surface texture and so has encouraged our wish to touch it—a childishness we have retained—so he has pierced it with holes feeling confident that we shall show the same almost instinctive curiosity. We shall know more for having used these basic methods of inquiry, not of course about the human anatomy but of the sculptured stone.

There is a vast range of possibility between a Calder mobile and a Moore reclining figure. The multitude of possibilities is even more apparent if one lists also the materials, the novel alongside the traditional, prefabricated metals, glass, plastics, cast metals, wrought iron, terracotta, wood and stone. The contemporary sculptor is his own craftsman for all except the most elaborate castings: it is from this constant handling of materials that discoveries and subtleties of surface and shape come.

Contemporary sculpture is gradually establishing its place as a public art, though on very different terms from those that it enjoyed in the past. The sculpture on the façade of a Gothic cathedral proclaimed the spiritual church within, and the equestrian statue of a ruler from his central position in a city square imposed his authority even on the shapes of the buildings that rimmed the square. Today it is only around a few large buildings, or complexes of buildings, or in parks that we move slowly enough to *see* sculpture; congestion on sidewalks is as effective

Fig. 95: CONSTRUCTION. *Naum Gabo. Rotterdam. 1960. Welded steel—(Courtesy, The Netherlands Consulate General).*

as rapid transportation in limiting our seeing. The design of modern architecture is such that sculpture has no fixed position relative to it. In the asymmetrical compositions characteristic of modern plans, a piece of sculpture can be moved around to balance or accent the whole effect or as a focus of interest to direct the way to entrances. Naum Gabo's CONSTRUCTION (Fig. 95) in front of a large departmental store in Rotterdam is a vivid contrast to the boxlike structure of the store, the contrast redounding to the advantage of both. Placed at a little distance from the entrances and well out from the store, it commands the attention of people coming down the street. Its appeal is simply pleasurable—it is hard to think of a theme suitable to departmental stores—and it is in fact hardly more than an elegant advertising sign. Henry Moore has made much public sculpture: one showing a reclining figure is to be seen on the lawn before the UNESCO building in Paris. Placed upon the ground like a great stone resting on mother earth, the human form is pertinent to a site in front of the headquarters. This is recognized by the central position relative to the curved face of the building: it is the centre of the arc described around it, as man is the centre of the activities sponsored by UNESCO.

The number of examples of the effective use of modern sculpture adorning modern architecture is still small. Sculpture has necessarily had to wait until modern architecture itself gained general acceptance, and this has been taking place only in the last twenty years. A wider public use has been in parks where the natural setting poses fewer artistic problems in regard to siting. The park can easily become an outdoor art gallery for leisurely viewing. Sculpture's frequent appearances in private collections and in public museums, round out the list of modern uses of it and bear witness to the rapid recovery of its position among the principal visual arts.

Fig. 96: LAKE SHORE DRIVE APARTMENTS, *Chicago.*
Mies van der Rohe. 1950-1952—(Photo by Wayne
Andrews).

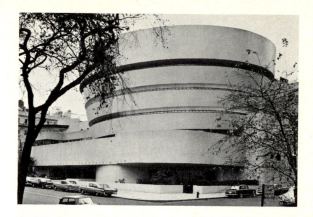

Fig. 97: GUGGENHEIM MUSEUM, *New York. F. L. Wright. 1959—(Courtesy, The Solomon R. Guggenheim Museum).*

Chapter V

MODERN MOVEMENTS IN ARCHITECTURE

Until the end of the nineteenth century, the leaders in architecture had been English, French, or Americans. In the twentieth century, they were joined by Germans, Dutch, Scandinavians, Italians, Brazilians, and Japanese to create a world-wide new expression. Historical styles continued to hamper the general acceptance of contemporary forms. Until after World War II the clientele, save for isolated and unimportant public bodies and a handful of private companies, was a scattering of modern-minded individuals. The depressed economic situation of the 1930's reduced all activity but did more to destroy the standards of the nineteenth century than blight new growth. The post World-War-II world is much closer to accepting architecture in its role as an art in constant adjustment to modern needs. All kinds of commissions are now available, and a large body of experience is at hand on which the architect can draw to maintain a high standard.

The century began in the midst of the Art Nouveau, a wide-spread and short-lived art form, employed more in the applied arts and interior decoration than in architecture. In this, it was very much like the Rococo. Art Nouveau made no use of structural or material innovations but it demonstrated in its extreme examples, the readiness of architects at the beginning of the century to put forward their own private ideas in complete defiance of the past. Their attitude entirely justified the name it was given—"the new art".

Fig. 98: CASA MILÁ, *Barcelona. A. Gaudi. 1905-1907—(Courtesy, Mas-Art Reference Bureau).*

The CASA MILÁ, (Fig. 98) an apartment block, by Antoni Gaudi (1852-1926) built in Barcelona 1905-07 is, for the Art Nouveau, an exceptionally large building. There is a complete avoidance of straight lines or regular curves on the exterior. Inside, there is hardly a room with two walls at right angles to each other. The railings, which protect the apartment balconies, are a tangled mass of wrought iron looking like seaweed clinging to the smooth face of water-eroded rock. A challenge to all past architecture, the building is still today a disturbing sight. There are other buildings by Gaudi in Barcelona, and their appearance adds interest to the townscape; but, it is impossible to imagine a whole city built after such a conception. As an architectural style, Art Nouveau stood against the current of the times, and the Casa Milá remains a monument to the uncontrolled private expression of the individual artist.

Meanwhile, a very great architect had come upon the scene, Frank Lloyd Wright (1867-1961), the product of the vigorous and isolated Chicago developments of the last quarter of the preceding century. Trained under Louis Sullivan, he played the role of pioneer and

Fig. 99: ROBIE HOUSE, *Chicago. F. L. Wright. 1909–(Courtesy, H. Allen Brooks, Dept. of Fine Art, University of Toronto).*

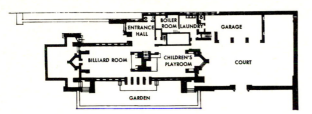

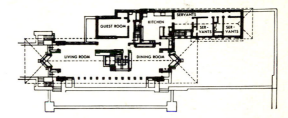

Fig. 99A: *Plan of ground floor and first floor of the* ROBIE HOUSE, *Chicago.*

prophet rather than that of leader. After 1910, the year his work was made known to Europe, his influence became international. By then he had designed a group of moderately large private homes mostly in and near Chicago that have been named his "Prairie Houses". The ROBIE HOUSE, Chicago, 1909, (Fig. 99), built of long, thin Roman brick is the largest. The house extends outward from a solid vertical core formed by the stairs and fireplace chimneys, the outward extensions exaggerated by broad terraces and overhanging eaves. The roofs, having the least possible slope, are virtually horizontally slabs slipped in between the strata of terraces and storeys. The windows are ranged in series to elaborate the horizontal emphasis. In effect, there is no front, but in walking around the house one is acutely aware of a continuously changing asymmetrical massing of rectangular forms, solidly grouped at the centre and thrust out into space at the edges. In Wright's mind, the dominant horizontality of the house identified the building and its inhabitants with the flat prairie land, the core of fireplaces with the basic sheltering function of a home, and the flung-out porches with the expansiveness of the mid-west American temperament. Obviously, the Robie House goes far beyond simple utility as a home, and, as clearly, it has no ties to past styles.

Internally, the rooms lie around the core of fireplaces and stair, one room slipping into the next, functionally and visually, and drawing interest onward. Ceiling timbers, fireplaces, etc., are exceedingly massive. Much emphasis is placed upon these structural members to convey a kind of pioneer permanence to the building. One feels that life in the Robie House was meant to be both ample and informal. Many of the preliminary stages in the development of this type of house had been taken in the holiday cottages built for wealthy Easterners in the preceding generation; the Robie House perfected the union of building and external physical environment without, and, of one living area to another within.

Twenty years later, the Swiss-French architect, Le Corbusier (1888-1965), designed the SAVOYE HOUSE (1929-30) (Fig. 100) in Poissy, a suburb of Paris. The building stands in a field, but it is cut off from the ground by its boxlike shape and the insulation of its elevation on columns. At ground level, and back under the shade of the upper storey, is a carport and service quarters, the presence of which is played down by the dark painting of the ground floor walls. Each wall of the box is identical; like a Greek temple, the Savoye House is very self-contained. What space there is exterior to the living quarters proper is precisely controlled—an enclosed patio on the second floor and a screened sundeck above reached by a ramp. All shapes are severely geometrical though by no means are all shapes rectangular, the walls, smooth and flat, the colour a uniform white. The whole is a weightless box in appearance, perched atop slender columns. At first sight, nothing can be more different from the Robie House, the one solidly based on the earth, its parts thrust out into the air around it as though trying to get into nature surrounding it; the other aloof, compacted and, save for the sky above, withdrawing its inhabitants from an experience of nature at close hand. The differences are not as they would have been, in the nineteenth century, between two historical styles. They result from differences of personality of the architects, American and Frenchman, and they are united by certain basic similarities peculiar to the twentieth century. The glass walls, which extend visually the living space into the patio and give glimpses of walls and ramps beyond, melt away the sense of enclosure just as Wright's interiors are not limited but give glimpses into further rooms whose walls appear through openings as parts of the composition.

Savoye House represents the first expansion of modern architecture known as the International Style. Centred in Holland, Germany, and France between 1920-35, it is closely related to contemporary developments in painting and sculpture, represented by Mondrian and Gabo. Le Corbusier's definition of a house as a "machine for living" is exemplified by the sparse neatness of the structure.

J. Rietveld's SCHROEDER HOUSE, Utrecht (Fig. 101) is a compact version of this International Style, having the appearance of slabs of concrete stacked to enclose rooms. Small balconies and windows provide many connections to the outside. Viewed from a distance the rectangular planning of the exterior is very similar to the paintings of Mondrian.

The refinement of all details extended to the furnishings as well, and even to the planning of these furnishings. Ultimately, rigidity resulted from such complete adherence to a programme, and the International Style is a finished chapter in modern art. Besides Le Corbusier, its most distinguished practitioners were Gropius, Mies van der Rohe, and J. J. P. Oud.

More important today is the kind of housing that will shelter the populations of large cities who cannot be accommodated in single family dwellings. The row house and the apartment are the only solutions. Even while they were building separate homes, the principal European architects were concerning themselves with a problem that in heavily-populated Europe was perhaps more pressing than it is elsewhere and to which they had also been drawn because, as architects, they felt a strong sense of responsibility to society. The high-rise apartment is the result: already in Europe this is so, and eventually elsewhere all urban housing will be of this type. The very large size of these units, bringing home to the observer the degree to which the individual is lost in the mass of the modern city, constitutes a peculiarly twentieth-century artistic problem. A variety of solutions has been offered.

Fig. 100: SAVOYE HOUSE, *Poissy, France. Le Corbusier. 1929-1930— (Courtesy, H. Allen Brooks, Dept. of Fine Art, University of Toronto).*

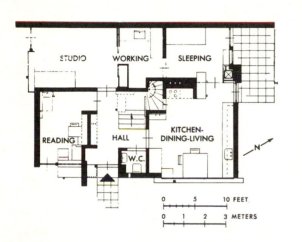

STUDIO WORKING SLEEPING

READING   HALL   KITCHEN-
                   DINING-LIVING
           W.C.

N

0   5   10 FEET
0 1   2   3 METERS

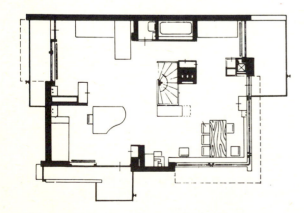

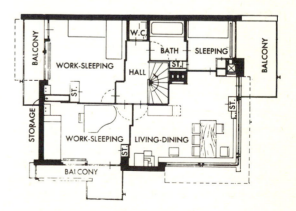

BALCONY   WORK-SLEEPING   W.C.   BATH   SLEEPING   BALCONY
STORAGE   ST.   HALL   ST.   ST.
           WORK-SLEEPING   LIVING-DINING
           ST.
           BALCONY

Fig. 101: SCHROEDER HOUSE, *Utrecht, Holland. J. Rietveld. 1924. Exterior view and plan of three floors. (Photo by Jan Versnel).*

The apartment block can become a little world, providing self-sufficiency and protection against the endless extent of the city beyond, as in Le Corbusier's UNITÉ D'HABITATION (Fig. 102), Marseilles (1946-1952). The peril of monotony by reason of size has been met through variations of fenestration corresponding to differing interior use and by the exaggeration of minor utilitarian features, the stair at one end for example, or the service housings on the roof as large sculpturelike concrete forms. In this "Habitation" and all his latest buildings, Le Corbusier has abandoned the effect of lightness that marked his earlier work. The piers are sturdy legs upon which rests the building cast roughly in concrete, its two long walls for the most part deeply pitted by massive balconies to suggest a wall at least five feet thick. There are painted panels of different colours on the sides of the balcony partitions, tinting as it were the warm tone of the rough concrete. In a community visually defined by the container of the building, the apartment, anchored on the site, proclaims permanence and security to passerby and inhabitant alike.

The apartments themselves are of two storeys so that the inhabitant has the freedom and variety of living in three dimensions, the two-storeyed living room giving greater scope to the quarters. From it, on alternative levels the apartment-dweller looks beyond the shadowed balcony to the Mediterranean or the Alps and the brilliance of the southern sun. The apartment extends through to the other side in one storey. The faces of the building show, alternatively, fronts and backs of apartments, their presence indicated by the very different window arrangement in broad and narrow zones. The vertically louvred strip near the middle of the elevation corresponds to a one-storeyed, inside shopping area at that level; the block becomes thereby a self-contained island of population having its services in the very middle of the building. The roof is a recreation area; the various housings of elevator and ventilating machinery are like simple pieces of sculpture spacing out and varying the view across the roof deck.

The building contains 337 apartments of 23 varieties capable of housing from one to five people, a shopping area, a lecture hall, a gymnasium, and a school, in short, a complete community. The designer has served as architect, town planner, and community organizer. Everything is taken care of just as in the modern welfare state.

Quite the opposite is the intention of the German-American architect, Mies van der Rohe (b. 1888) in his LAKESHORE APARTMENTS, (1949-1951) (Fig. 96), Chicago. The two identical blocks are erected on stilts, in such a way as to resemble a cube, the height of which appears, to the viewer, to be the principal, but not the dominating, factor. Great care extends to the window shapes and their grouping and to the proportions of skeleton and filling material. The inheritance of the International Style is obvious, but there is an important difference expressed in a rigid symmetry of grouping (e.g., three groups of four windows on the ends, five of four on the side) and in the balance of dimensions. Quite apart from their function as housing, viewers cannot help but consider them as beautiful harmonious shapes that compel attention. The asymmetry of accent of the International Style is gone and with it the tensions and restlessness of a constantly shifting attention. At the same time, it is clear that the building is a human hive in which all cells are alike. Mies' apartments are an acceptance of the anonymity of the city and also an attempt to make of them objects of beauty for the outsider. It is difficult to imagine a greater contrast between two works of art than that between the Unité d'Habitation and the Lakeshore Apartments. Traceable to differences of climate, local and national traditions of housing, economic variants, and the personalities of the two architects, the buildings reveal the range of possibilities in one of the most critical and, therefore, stimulating situations of the present time.

The problem of the housing of large numbers of people is partly satisfied by the high-rise apartment; but it is increasingly evident that whole areas of older cities and new towns must be developed to take care of the crush of population. Several architects of prominence have been attracted to the designing of whole cities. Le Corbusier, for instance, sketched a complete rehabilitation of the centre of Paris in 1925, but until after World War II commissions were scarce. This problem has become the greatest test of the architectural designer today. To solve it he must collaborate with a team of civil engineers, economists, geographers. If he is to be successful, he must obtain the highest degree of material comfort, and provide a large measure of recreative and spiritual facilities, in the most compact manner possible, for a community that may number up to 50,000 people. Complete units have been designed in the past, e.g., the St. Gall monastery, as well as many Baroque cities, but there was always a focal point to which the parts could be related and organized. The modern unit, having for its goal the material and spiritual well-being of a very great variety of citizens, has, as an objective, nothing like a church or palace, a god to worship, or a king to obey. Two centuries of intermittent experiment with asymmetry in composition plus special concentration of all artists, architects, painters, and sculptors, on the problems of design in space have taught the creators of these new subdivisions and towns to combine a wide range of buildings to give a constantly changing variety of experience to those moving about the community (Fig. 103). If there are, as yet, no masterpieces to point to, it must be remembered that the problem is new and particularly demanding. It has been made more so by the near disappearance of those single objects of special attention that once held together a whole community, namely, churches, royal palaces, seats of government, the squares as settings for statues, or great fountains. A city's silhouette was once memorable, like that of Siena, where church and state appeared over the house tops in the dome of the cathedral, and in the belfry of the Palazzo Publico. Today, a shapely group of apartment blocks would replace such buildings.

Inevitably contemporary architects have been called upon to design public buildings, not only to house services but to have a higher duty of "standing for" the invisible values of religion, political order, and education. In the International Style phase of the 1920's the few churches, town halls or schools, which were commissioned, were almost totally unrecognizable in traditional terms. The schools were the most successful, however, because there was less tradition to shake off.

The nineteenth century had wavered between the notion of the pursuit of knowledge as a withdrawn and cloistered activity for which the Gothic was historically the most suited style and the idea that a Classic or Baroque form best signified the majesty and importance to the State of the pursuit of knowledge. In the twentieth century, the stress on educational process rather than on the body of knowledge has put more emphasis on the school as instrument or machine. The BAUHAUS, DESSAU, (Fig. 104), in Germany (1925-26) is the most famous modern school. Built by Walter Gropius (b. 1883) who was also the director, it housed an art training programme in which a successful attempt was made to reconcile art and the techniques of the machine age. The Bauhaus looks like a modern factory; and in fact Gropius had been a factory builder of distinction before World War I. The resemblance was appropriate, bearing in mind the programme of the school.

It consisted of workshops, class rooms, administrative quarters and studio apartments for the students. Each function is separated in a three-armed building, and the administration section is the bridge connecting the parts. The glass-walled workshops are the most famous unit and provide the first example of the extreme demonstration that walls may be filling surfaces only and quite transparent. This wing is a demonstration of factory efficiency of lighting and a showcase for the key claim of Gropius' teaching, namely, to reconcile art and modern techniques. The classroom section is less distinctive, and the residence portion by its greater height and balconied walls is distinguished from the working area. Though practical utilitarian considerations deeply influenced the architect, the design would not have been so memorable had not Gropius been able to avail himself of the general interest in geometric formal compositions on surface and in depth which preoccupied the 1920's everywhere and is known as Cubism in painting and sculpture and as the International Style in architecture.

This complex of building has no single line of approach; entrances are not emphasized though they are conveniently placed for communication. From any position, the Bauhaus is seen to equal advantage as a grouping of cubic units with at least two of the main units related in asymmetrical composition at different points in space. Many of the boundaries of the units are made ambiguously transparent through the use of glass. Everything is relative to something else: the only constant is change or exploration of the building's appearance. To people who believed that the purpose of education demanded a constant adaptation to a changing environment, the Bauhaus was the symbol of those invisible ideals it housed.

Fig. 104: BAUHAUS, *Dessau, Germany. W. Gropius. 1925-1926—(Courtesy, The Museum of Modern Art, New York).*

The school as an educational factory may offend: it is hardly more extreme than the thought of a school as a pseudo-palace of learning. At present, the search is on to discover a less factorylike appearance so that education may have its own identity in architecture. The notion that education is a temporary withdrawal from the mainstream in order better to understand what is seen from a little distance will work changes, and so will the contemporary faith amounting almost to a religion that only by a constant stress on education can we, as a civilization, survive. This is quite apparent to those who visit the grounds of the Massachusetts Institute of Technology, the most modern scientific school in the world. There, all manner of unfamiliar forms appear, including dormitories, serpentine in plan. If these various essays into modern form seem to bear little relation to one another it is because the direction to be taken is still not at all clear.

One of the strangest of these buildings at M.I.T. is a chapel. Since World War II, architects have been called upon to build many houses of God, and they have responded to the challenge with an extraordinary release of imagination. Here the practical considerations, which have played such a role in private and mass housing and even in schools, do not operate and the developments of the first forty years in modern architecture have not been so strictly binding.

Fig. 105: NOTRE DAME, *Le Raincy, Paris, France. A. Perret. 1922-1923—(Photo by G. E. Kidder Smith, New York).*

It was already realized in the 1920's that the weightlessness of modern construction and the possibilities of complete freedom of lighting presented the architect with technical means not unlike the situation in the Middle Ages. Our modern preoccupation with both real and artificial light has given us an interest in, and a control over, this medium of great value to the designer of churches. Auguste Perret (1874-1954) designed in reinforced concrete, the Church of LE RAINCY in the suburbs of Paris, 1925. The exterior is rather bare in appearance; its interior (Fig. 105), covered by nearly flat vaults perched on slender colonettes, is lit by windowed walls as thoroughly glazed as a Gothic cathedral itself. The structural and decorative forms are those suggested by the material itself, though the reminiscences, particularly of the Middle Ages, suggest the ties of tradition. The apse is shallow, the columns punctuate but do not break up the space, the windows hang a translucent curtain around the hall and illuminate all parts of the room with equal brilliance.

Fig. 106: CHAPEL. *Ronchamp, France. Le Corbusier. 1950-1955—(Courtesy, H. Allen Brooks, Dept. of Fine Art, University of Toronto).*

Since World War II, the congregational nature of churches and synagogues has been much emphasized in design by the frequent use of a central plan. The distinction from ordinary domestic or commercial architecture has been effected by the use of dome or eccentrically vaulted forms reminiscent of Byzantine or Gothic forms, but made in cast concrete and laminated woods. The most extraordinary example of the change in religious architecture is the pilgrimage chapel of RONCHÁMP (Fig. 106) in eastern France built by Le Corbusier in 1950-55. Built on a high hill, it bears no resemblance to any church of tradition and looks more like a primitive menhir of the pre-Christian Celtic peoples. It is a place so strange as to have a kind of magical quality of its own. The roof, like a great stone, rests on a perforated base, and, standing beside it is a knoblike tower. The per-

forations are windows dotted about the walls in an arbitrary fashion, revealing the thickness of the walls. Within, the space is cavelike and ill-defined by reason of the curving walls and haphazard lighting coming through embrasures so deep as to make the outside seem very remote. The materials of the building are as permanent in appearance as they are primitive, and this applies to all the church furnishings as well. The emotion that Ronchamp's architect hopes to arouse is one of wonder and holy fear, felt once by hermits and pilgrims to strange places. Only among those who are deliberately fleeing from the world can we expect to find sympathy for this refuge. Similarly, the architecture of the chapel has no obvious point of contact with the architecture of the world beyond the hill on which it stands.

Ronchamp is of reinforced concrete, a medium for building that has long been popular in those parts of Europe where labour costs are relatively small, and the expense great of the steel for steel frame construction. Permitting as it does more eccentric shapes than steel, it is thus a freer medium for design. Frank Lloyd Wright's GUGGENHEIM MUSEUM, New York, (Fig. 97) contains curved form shockingly different from the cubic shapes of nearby apartment blocks. As in the Gaudi CASA MILÁ, the occasional distinctive building calling for special consideration by reason of its place or function, can be assimilated to the modern townscape. It is more difficult to imagine whole cities in this kind of dress.

The design, in terms of modern architecture of public buildings has been most difficult. The state, whether national or local, is complex in its many functions and difficult for people to grasp except in terms of national leaders, men of superhuman powers but still of human physical scale. The temples of republics or the mediaeval or baroque royal palaces, which served for the nineteenth century, are physically inadequate to contain the thousands of employees of the state; as symbols of government, they are also obsolete. Three great capital building complexes have been realized of late years and the services of the best modern architects were obtained as governments came to see the need for an impressive and enduring image of government. Brasilia, the new capital of Brazil; Chandigarh the provincial capital of Punjab, India; the United Nations building, New York; all of them were designed by Le Corbusier or by his followers. The object in all cases is to create, by utilizing the full possibilities of modern techniques, a memorable building or group of buildings, which as the symbols of the state proclaim both modernity and permanence.

The United Nations building, New York, (Fig. 107), is memorable—the simple huge shape of the office block would see to that. It is a combined enterprise of architects, obviously dominated by the ideas of Le Corbusier. The analysis of the kind of building needed goes back to the Swiss students' residence for the University of Paris, built by Le Corbusier in 1932, where the design consisted of a slab dormitory block, long, high, and narrow, joined to a low building housing the common rooms, offices, and foyer. The first represents the many separate rooms and private lives of the student; the second, his communal activities. The first is set up on piers and isolated from direct intrusion; the second can be entered quite easily from outside.

The United Nations building follows this line of thinking; the Secretariat is in the high block, the Assembly and foyers in the lower. Size alone would make the building prominent, its isolated position keeping other buildings at a distance where they seem even smaller by comparison. The employment of glass in an immense surface, the extreme contrast of horizontal and vertical units, cubic and curved shapes—all of these add up to a striking image easily recalled. As a capital building, it is a new concept, giving form to both the legislative and administrative activities of governments. The legislative section is easily accessible to the public moving to the halls and committee rooms through a setting of grandeur; the administrative section is isolated, housing thousands busy in the machinery of running the United Nations.

In Le Corbusier's subsequent essay toward a modern capital, Chandigarh, the various functions of government are housed in separate buildings in a composition in which no one element is central and dominating. Whereas the United Nations building strikes the beholder as thoroughly contemporary and therefore international, Chandigarh, as the capital of a province of Pakistan, hints at, though it does not imitate, the massive fortress and palace architecture of Moslem India.

Fig. 107: UNITED NATIONS BUILDING. *W. K. Harrison and an Inter-national Advisory Committee including Le Corbusier. New York. 1949-1951—(Courtesy, United Nations).*

Fig. 108: ROCKEFELLER CENTER, *New York. Various architects. 1931-1940—*
(Courtesy, Rockefeller Center Inc.).

Fig. 109: Mrs. Thomas Boylston. *J. S. Copley. Fogg Museum, Cambridge, Massachusetts. 1766. 50½″ x 40½″ —(Courtesy, Harvard University).*

Chapter VI

AMERICAN ART

The Colonial Era

ARCHITECTURE

The arts in the colonies, from the French in Quebec, to the Spaniards in South America were transplanted from Europe. Whatever the newcomers found of native origin they destroyed or ignored, but it was more difficult to dismiss the differences in climates and materials that made for change between Europe and America.

The position of the arts in the various colonies reflects the relation between colonies and homeland. In New Spain, the close and constant supervision of a government intent on extending the Old World to the New resulted in a truly imperial art magnificently represented in the buildings of Church and State. With less vigour, the French government in Canada followed the same policy. In each case, it was merely the extension of an attitude to the arts already established at home in Europe. The

English in America were in a different position. They came as independent adventurers often determined to be free of interference from England where the arts were in a critical condition. From the beginning of the seventeenth century down to the 1660's, the Puritans in England had effectively disrupted the arts, and parliamentary opposition to absolutism had destroyed the power of monarchy that once had been the greatest supporter of the arts.

The colonists themselves represented various shades of opinion; the Puritans in New England were as opposed to the arts that they deemed immoral as the gentleman adventurers in Virginia were convinced of their necessity. To all, however, architecture was the primary art; painting was limited to portraiture; sculpture had almost no place at all. It had not been much different in the England they had left.

Fig. 110: WHIPPLE HOUSE, *Ipswich, Massachusetts. Seventeenth century—(Photo by Frank O. Branzetti and courtesy of HABS, Library of Congress, Washington, D.C.).*

The WHIPPLE HOUSE at Ipswich (Fig. 110), near Boston, is characteristic of New England's seventeenth-century house. The method of framing the building is English, also the plan and elevation, and even the clapboard siding could be found in England. The core of chimneys in the middle provided fireplaces for rooms on either side on the ground and upper floors. What few embellishments the building had were part of an unquestioned old-fashioned tradition brought over from England. It was only in the late nineteenth century that these sturdy, practical buildings were again of interest to architects; the eighteenth century quickly outgrew them.

In the Virginia colony, there was a shade more ostentation in the early plantation houses, and there were also differences in planning as a consequence of the milder climate. The chimneys could be placed at the ends of the house, not in the middle, giving a more varied and massive appearance to the exterior. In New Amsterdam, now New York, slight Dutch details were visible. From the beginning, regionalism, arising from differing European traditions, local materials and climatic conditions, was a factor in American architectural history.

In the northern colonies, the principal building was the meetinghouse, used first, as a church, and, secondly, as a place of town business. This was natural enough in a community whose daily life was dominated by religion. Only one such building, the OLD SHIP MEETINGHOUSE, HINGHAM, (Fig. 111), has survived from the seventeenth century. Square in plan, boxlike in elevation, and topped by a belfry, amply lit on all sides with great windows, having galleries on three sides so that all could gather close about the pulpit, the meetinghouse was as defiant of ecclesiastical formalism as the dwellings of the Puritans were the preservers of the English domestic tradition. Plain as was the meeting-house, it was the most important structure in every town. It was to be expected that a sect as radical as the Calvinistic Protestants would practise their faith in a new and revolutionary setting. In backward regions and along the frontier of settlement, this simple setting persisted through the eighteenth century.

At the beginning of the eighteenth century, the first stage of adaptation to the wilderness was past, the prosperity of seaport towns was evident, and, in the northern colonies, the hold of extreme Puritanism was broken. On all levels, connections with England were strengthened. The arts benefited by the change. A sign of the times is the foundation of Williamsburg, the capital of Virginia, on a carefully-planned site in

Fig. 111: OLD SHIP MEETING HOUSE, *Hingham, Massachusetts. 1681 — (Photo by Frank O. Branzetti and courtesy of HABS, Library of Congress, Washington, D.C.).*

Fig. 112: WESTOVER *(Byrd Mansion), Virginia. River front. c.1730-1734—* *(Courtesy, Library of Congress, Washington, D.C.).*

which the legislative building, the governor's palace and the college of William and Mary were major points of architectural interest. WESTOVER (1726) (Fig. 112), in the same colony, is the first private mansion so arranged as to have both park and road fronts, a symmetrical arrangement of flanking outbuildings and an elaborate doorway trimmed with carved stone shipped from England. To the visitor, the breadth of this façade made Westover impressive; to the host, the stretch of the wings seemed to embrace his property; to all, the building had the air of an English gentleman's country estate, although a modest one.

In New England, where outbuildings were lacking, since all services were massed together in the main part of the house for the sake of warmth in winter, the continued use of clapboarding produced a variation much less English in appearance than the Southern houses that had many outbuildings. Inside, the plan was pretty much the same in all regions, namely, a large central hall out of which rose an elaborately carved staircase to the bedrooms above. On either side of the hall were two rooms, the proportions of which were studied for harmony and had panellings and mouldings, fireplaces and overmantles as ornamentally splendid as possible. This splendour was borrowed from carpenters' manuals published in England, as were many of the house plans from more elaborate publications. These plans could be used by builders fresh out from England or trained in America, often under the instruction of amateur gentlemen designers. Like his English counterpart, the educated American was often a man of taste, trained by reading and even travel, and ready to prove his experience by essays into architecture. Such men were America's first architects.

Fig. 113: KING'S CHAPEL, *Boston, Massachusetts. P. Harrison. Interior looking towards the altar. 1739-1754—(Photo by Wayne Andrews).*

The first to distinguish himself was Peter Harrison (1715-1775), born and educated in England, a resident of Newport, Rhode Island, successful merchant in the English trade, and, on the side, designer of two churches, a synagogue, a library and a public office block, besides private houses. All betray their source in the great folios of Italian Renaissance architecture and their English derivatives and are of a quality comparable to the best provincial English work that is, as is all provincial art a little old-fashioned but sound in design. KING'S CHAPEL, Boston (1749-1758) (Fig. 113), by Harrison, is a great change from the meeting-house of the preceding century. It is fashionable in that it follows elegant church types of England, represented by Gibbs' St. Martin's-in-the-Fields. It goes back to the longitudinal plan and is scaled up in size by the use of paired Corinthian columns. The stiff, plain Puritanism has disappeared. Culturally, at least, the New Englander of the eighteenth century was more attached to homeland than had been his grandfather.

The most famous and among the last of these gentlemen architects was Thomas Jefferson, the third president of the United States. Beginning as the designer of his own home, MONTICELLO (Fig. 114), he was in the first generation of the republic a kind of unofficial adviser on public architecture for the new nation, and ended his career with the plan of the University of Virginia. Monticello had started as a design from Palladio, having a two-level porch front but in its completed form was on a grander scale. A low dome tops a building whose front and back entrances are temple porticoes, but the impressiveness of these classic motifs is lessened by the pretty distractions of such detail as the oval windows in the base of the dome, and the complicated shapes of the ends of the building. The interior is like the exterior, an effort to be both stately and domestic at the same time, an architectural equivalent to Jefferson's own republican notion of his public duties and private rights.

The style illustrated by Monticello is usually labelled the "Federal". In slightly less grand a fashion, it was much used in the Boston area for the homes of wealthy merchants. A domestic architecture of elegance, the Federal was soon crowded out by the more massive forms of Neo-Classicism.

PAINTING

In the English colonies, the art of painting followed the same path, from simple utility to an imitative elegance. Until the mid-eighteenth century, portraiture was singularly devoid of decorative value or interpretative intention. The portraitist, or limner as he was called, had a place, if a lowly one, in the colonial world in supplying collections of family portraits as dear to the American man of easy circumstances as to his English counterpart. Rigidly-set solemn faces bear witness to an inadequate talent and a serious-minded sitter. A likeness was all that was required.

With the beginning of the eighteenth century, the demand for more elegance, which had appeared in architecture, had its parallel in the arrival of better-trained artists from Europe.

Fig. 114: MONTICELLO, *Charlottesville, Virginia. T. Jefferson. Garden front.*
1763-1809—(Courtesy, Virginia Chamber of Commerce. Photo by Flournoy.).

They settled in Boston, Newport, New York and Philadelphia, their presence preparing the way for the first American artists of genuine merit. The best of this new generation of native born artists was John Singleton Copley (1738-1815), of Boston, foster son of an immigrant artist. When as a young man he sent a portrait of his half-brother Henry Pelham to an exhibition in London, the quality was so great as to arouse Sir Joshua Reynold's interest, but it was not until 1775 that Copley went to live in London. By then, he had enjoyed nearly twenty years as the best and most fashionable painter in the colonies. In his portrait, MRS. THOMAS BOYLSTON, 1766 (Fig. 109), the wife of a Harvard professor and, therefore, a member of the best society of Boston, the drapes and column, the customary accessories of contemporary English portraiture are flat like a stage-drop, but the lady herself, her dress and the chair are to the last detail plainly before us. The light and shadow do not obscure the catalogue of appearances or conceal or flatter the facts of age. This picture and most of Copley's other portraits show people a little angular and stiff in pose and with a firm set to jaw. As a successful portrait painter, Copley painted his sitters as they wished to be seen, fashionably up-to-date but firm in their principles. At the same time in England, Reynolds and Gainsborough stressed wit and dash in their portraits: Copley's sitters were of sterner stuff.

Fig. 115: DEATH OF WOLFE. *B. West. National Gallery of Canada, Ottawa. 1770.*
59½″ x 84″. A replica is in the Canadiana Gallery, Royal Ontario Museum,
Toronto—(Courtesy, The National Gallery of Canada, Ottawa.).

The other American painter to attain prominence, though without the same talent, was Benjamin West (1738-1820). For an artistic education, this gifted Pennsylvanian was sent to Europe, from which he never returned. As George III's favourite, he enjoyed great success, chiefly as a painter of history. His DEATH OF WOLFE (Fig. 115) initiated a series of large historical canvases by European and American painters extending well into the next century. Before this, there had been only a handful of paintings detailing historical events. The time had come when people were aroused by the examples of history as a guide to conduct and action, and the death of Wolfe was both an excellent example of public conduct and a reminder of the possibilities of a British Empire.

Though it purports to be a description of an event, and West investigated accounts of the battle, it is in fact many single, careful observations joined by a conventional scheme. The foreground is a deliberate artistic grouping well removed from the accidents of battle, the smoke of which rolling back reveals a new light to which the dying hero looks as to a great new dawn. The group is one carefully chosen from all ranks of the army and degrees of their acquaintance with the general in order to indicate the pervading grief and the differing

Fig. 118: U.S. Capitol, *Washington, D.C. B. H. Latrobe. Before 1812. Engraving showing the original design by Latrobe—(Courtesy, The Old Print Shop, New York).*

throughout the United States west to the Mississippi. Imaginative adaptation was necessary in many cases because stucco-covered brick, or more often wood, had to be substituted for the marble, used by the Greeks. The range and vitality of the Greek Revival in the United States made for a period of native growth in which the borrowings from Antiquity had more the function of stimuli than controls. Some local variations appeared. In the Southern states, the colonnades of the temple plan formed a protective porch screening against the tropical heat (Fig. 119); in the North, they darkened the interior and were in many instances confined to house fronts. Eighteenth - century American houses had nothing so impressive as this general use of columns but now in a democracy the importance conferred by a colonnade could be enjoyed even by those of moderate means.

Fig. 119: Taylor Grady House, *Athens, Georgia. c.1840—(Photo by Frederic D. Nichols and courtesy of HABS, Library of Congress, Washington, D.C.).*

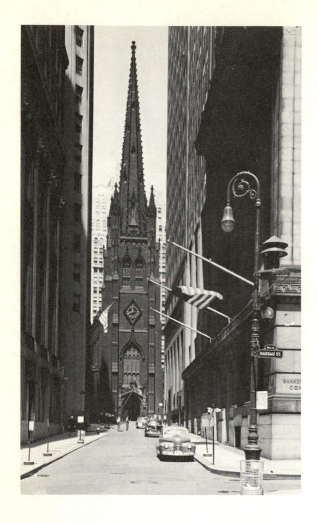

Fig. 120: TRINITY CHURCH, *Broadway and Wall Street, New York. R. Upjohn. 1846—(Photo by Wayne Andrews).*

The Gothic Revival made its appearance in the United States after the beginning of the century, but until the 1840's it was in no sense a competitor with the Greek Revival. The Middle Ages were very remote from America and were appreciated mainly through the works of such novelists as Sir Walter Scott. The religious enthusiasm that had marked an earlier period in England and the continent found other outlets in the United States. The Episcopal Church by reason of its connections with England was the first to use Gothic Revival extensively. Richard Upjohn (1802-1878), a trained architect and English emigrant, brought an up-to-date knowledge to the building of TRINITY CHURCH (Fig. 120), New York, 1846. Gothic cottages became immediately popular,

and the peaks of their roofs and high chimneys made ragged silhouettes against the sky. Planted about with trees in a "natural" park, the Gothic cottage provided a complete contrast to its Classic Revival neighbours. There was invention and adaptation in Gothic as well. The vertical wood siding often used had no mediaeval precedent, and the bargeboards were given over to a fantasy of carving rarely equalled in Europe.

In the 1840's also, and again from England, the Italian Villa made its appearance. A building in blocks asymmetrically composed around a tower of medium height, with round and square-headed windows, it was called Italian by reason of its Renaissance detail in eaves and door

Fig. 121: SMITHSONIAN INSTITUTE, *Washington, D.C. J. Renwick. 1846—(Courtesy, The Smithsonian Institute).*

frames. It was the style of a limited clientele, however, being confined to large houses of stone, brick, or stucco. Both the Greek revival and the Gothic were sufficiently assimilated that they could be used even in the smallest structures in even the cheapest material, wood.

Examples of other styles, currently sampled in Europe, were found in the United States also, though none with wide circulation. The most extraordinary is the SMITHSONIAN INSTITUTE, WASHINGTON (Fig. 121), designed by James Renwick and built between 1846-1855 in what is mostly Romanesque with touches of Gothic. If such a mixture seems strange for a natural science museum, it must be remembered that this was a new kind of building, that science itself was an exciting adventure, and that an almost fairyland jumble of towers was deemed appropriate to a conception of science as an exhibition of wonders. Being Romanesque,

moreover, it enjoyed the romantic appeal of the Middle Ages without being associated with the Ecclesiastical, the special province of the Gothic.

As in Europe, certain technological inventions of the 1840's and 1850's prepared the way for important later developments. The system of framing a wooden house, known as balloon construction, because it lightened the wall, freed the designer from the restrictions of earlier framing methods. Again, whole fronts of cast iron, made in units, could be bolted to the front of a building. The moulds in which the iron was cast might be one of numerous available styles, usually little related to what was behind them, but this new procedure helped establish the notion of a wall, as filling, without structural meaning for the building back of it. Finally, the elevator invented by Otis, made possible, after the Civil War, the skyward development of the American city.

Fig. 122: THE OXBOW OF THE CONNECTICUT. *T. Cole. Metropolitan Museum, New York. 1836. 39″ x 54″—(Courtesy, The Metropolitan Museum of Art. Gift of Mrs. Russell Sage, 1908).*

PAINTING

The huge success of landscape painting after the War of 1812 can be traced back in part to the great popularity of landscapes in England and the central position of nature in English poetry. If there had been a considerable time lag in the case of the Americans, it was because the eighteenth and early nineteenth centuries were bent on proclaiming the advance of civilization, not in finding art or poetry in a wilderness that extended to the seaboard. It was only with the establishment of an urban civilization that nature began to seem to offer contrasting attractions. Significantly, the first group of landscape painters worked in the Hudson River valley and the Catskill mountains, the nearest authentic romantic wilderness to the largest city in the United States, New York, where their best market was

to be found. The Hudson River School, as it is called, had almost a dozen artists, painting between 1820-1870, whose work, though originally including a majority of paintings made in the Hudson River valley, came to embrace much Appalachian landscape; around this nucleus was a good sprinkling of painters recording scenes from all over America and even abroad. The first in importance is Thomas Cole (1801-1848). The America he saw was a land of towering mountains, great forests and tumbling waters reached through a foreground tangle of shattered trees, the whole painted in a time-honoured convention of colours only vaguely based on observation. In THE OXBOW OF THE CONNECTICUT (Fig. 122), the battered tree, the shaggy hillside just beyond, and storm clouds at upper left, diagonally fill half the landscape, the other half of which is as full of quiet curving and spacious forms as the first is of violence. Cole has used the scene to describe the two faces of Nature, the one destructively wild, the other peaceful and cultivated. Other painters were less given to sermonizing on Nature, resting content with a careful account of its physical appearance into whose quiet spaces the viewer could withdraw from the world. As the pioneers moved westward to the Rockies, and the scale of nature grew larger in the mountains, the grandeur of this last frontier was called forth in landscapes, often of immense size. When, ultimately, artists felt they had exhausted the scenic possibilities of the United States, a few painters went to Europe, South America, and the Arctic to search out the highest mountains, the biggest volcanoes, or largest icebergs. The arm-chair traveller, who owned such a picture, asked nothing more of the painting than that it carry him off to the dreamland of adventure. This was the stage of landscape painting at the outbreak of the Civil War.

In the first half of the nineteenth century, there was also a good deal of reporting of fact as well as recording of the viewer's feelings in the face of nature. Trained topographical draughtsmen—many of the first of them English immigrants or visitors—passed through America recording the harbours, towns, rivers, mountains and anything else that might, when engraved and printed, be saleable to a European or American public in book form or single sheet. Facts were the immediate concern of draughtsmen who remained artists enough, however, to select and even exaggerate the more entertaining aspects of what they saw. From about 1830 on, the appearance, costumes and customs of the Indian were observed with the same enthusiasm for fact coupled with the usual prejudices about aborigines. It is rare that these records had much scientific or artistic merit; but, exceptionally, Audubon's THE BIRDS OF AMERICA had both. To John James Audubon (1785-1851), the frontier was its wild life, more especially its birds, his records of which this French-trained artist-naturalist between 1827-1837 published as THE BIRDS OF AMERICA. In

Fig. 123: CAROLINA PARROQUET. *J. J. Audubon. From "American Birds", engraved by R. Havell. 1827-1838. Coloured aquatint— (Courtesy, The New York Historical Society, New York).*

Europe, there had been a long history of scientific illustration originating in the Renaissance and having two characteristics: the clear description of specimens and their decorative arrangement on the printed page. For clarity, the space about the specimen was limited to the whiteness of the page, modelling in shadow reduced, contours emphasized, the silhouette stressed for decorativeness, and its relation to the rectangle of the page carefully studied. Audubon, heir to all these traditions, added an unusual knowledge of the birds in their natural habitat. The vitality of his CAROLINA PARROQUET (Fig. 123) is a gain both to scientific information and to the spectator's awareness of the image as art. Done originally in brilliant watercolours, they were translated into coloured engravings by

Fig. 124: FUR TRADERS DESCENDING THE MISSOURI. *G. C. Bingham. Metropolitan Museum of Art, New York. c.1845. 29″ x 36″—(Courtesy, The Metropolitan Museum of Art. Morris K. Jesup Fund, 1933).*

Robert Havell, Jr., an Englishman who further sharpened the two-dimensional pattern and increased its effectiveness as page decoration.

To Americans of the first half of the century, their own activities were as interesting as their physical environment. Genre painting, often quite closely patterned after the traditions of Dutch seventeenth-century painting, had a ready sale. Many artists who specialized in this medium had trained in Germany at the art school of Düsseldorf where a good education provided them with technical skill though it sheltered them from the new ideas forming in Paris. W. S. Mount (1807-1868) specialized in the idyllic farmyard scene so peacefully ordered as to make the owners of his pictures pine nostalgically for the countryside they had deserted for the commerce of the city. Another, George Caleb Bingham (1811-1879), lived in Missouri on the edge of the frontier. More ambitious than most genre painters, he wished to suggest the heroic greatness of the life led by the frontier peoples. In FUR TRADERS DESCENDING THE MISSOURI, (Fig. 124) the three occupants

Fig. 125: HOME TO THANKSGIVING. *Currier and Ives. Print after a painting by G. H. Durrie. 1862. Lithograph—(Courtesy, The Harry T. Peters Collection. Museum of The City of New York).*

of the canoe, tame fox, boy, and older man, are carefully isolated along the length of the boat to give equal emphasis to all three. The peaceful horizontal arrangement is seen in detail and emphatically against the misty indications of the broad river and distant shore. The composition is unusual and easily strikes into the memory. No painting can better describe, than does this picture, the empty silence in which the first travellers to the west found themselves nor the voyagers' confidence in the face of this endless land. Bingham had an interest in the region which went beyond recording merely its immediate life in art. He

finally quit painting to become an active political figure in his state.

In the first half of the century, almost every artist in America owed part of his income and much of his popularity to the medium of inexpensive prints (Fig. 125). Currier and Ives in New York were the most famous, if not the best, of the publishers. They provided, at a very low cost, reproductions of well-known paintings and many original designs, often assembling these in series of related subjects. The prints constituted a truly democratic form of art, in that they were inexpensive, widely distributed, informative as well as pleasing, and

Fig. 126: STOUGHTON HOUSE, *Cambridge, Massachusetts.*
H. H. Richardson. 1883—(Photo by Wayne Andrews).

mirrored the life with which their purchasers were most familiar, namely, their own.

Other evidences of democracy were at work colouring the taste of the United States in these years before the Civil War. One, John Rogers, had discovered the market for sculpture produced on a mass scale and had devised a mould from which he could extract dozens of copies of small groups cast in plaster. These were sold by sales catalogue to those who had already decorated their walls with framed Currier and Ives prints. To the American of the 1860's, the arts were very much at home in the United States; and though they were quite out of touch with what was going on in Europe their North American flavour was all to the individual American's liking.

The Era of Commercial Expansion

The Civil War brought great changes to the position of the arts in the United States. It had hastened the industrialization of the country, the development of the Middle West, and the growth of New York and Chicago. Great personal fortunes had come into existence, and were held by people untrained in taste and eager to establish themselves in the cosmopolitan worlds of the very rich. For three generations after 1870, the United States, in searching for art, set its sights eastward to Europe—the very opposite of that withdrawal from Europe that had gone on between 1820 and 1860.

ARCHITECTURE

The character of the new America can be illustrated by the situation in architecture. Before the Civil War, the public building, the visible evidence of the republican state, was the most important type of structure. After the Civil War, the commercial building, as the monument to free enterprise and the capitalist economy, was the object of most architectural invention.

After the war, architecture underwent, in the next decade, its final debasement—the Napoleon III adaptation of baroque. Grandeur, expressed by large quantities of ornament heaped on all openings, along the silhouette of the building and against the wall itself, satisfied the uncertain taste. Vulgar display gave way in the 1870's to a more refined exhibition of wealth and power. In New York and Newport, great houses imitative of Florentine palaces or castles along the Loire were built by architects trained in France to respect the forms of earlier architectural styles and ready to import into America not only styles but also European craftsmen to make their creations possible. The vast expenditure of wealth did not produce a cultivated patronage nor did it stimulate a wave of artistic creation. Yet, at the time that this blind path was being followed, sometimes in the same towns of the Atlantic seaboard, domestic architecture with a future was appearing. It had grown out of the imitation of Gothic irregularity once admired as picturesque and then seen as a method of obtaining a comfortable informality of interior rooms opening on verandahs. Houses built in this way could be large enough to suit the wealthiest client and yet retain a casual air. A large entrance hall housed the staircase, but was big enough to form part of the living-room into which it opened, and the dining-room and porches gave off it, too, allowing of easy movement about the downstairs and a feeling that most of the ground floor was one large space flowing from room to room. Many of the first examples of this new mode of planning were summer residences where one would expect a less formal mode of life, even for the wealthy.

The opening stage was called the Shingle Style from the preferred way of finishing the exterior. An example by the most famous architect of the day, H. H. Richardson, is the STOUGHTON HOUSE (Fig. 126), Cambridge, Massachusetts. The plan and elevation are irregular, and the exterior surface is remarkably plain, a sharp contrast to the heavily ornamented exteriors of those houses that followed the various revival styles. There are no elaborate eaves, fancy window or door frames. The shingles provide a textured surface, and the windows by careful spacing give variety of interest to the walls. In New England, the use of this kind of shingle sheathing was traditional for simple cottages on Cape Cod. On other houses, verandahs were important elements: these, too, were an old American element with no European roots. Internally, there was a good deal of wood visible in panelling of walls, screens, and beamed ceilings. The shingle style in fact was a triumph of an historically American material, wood, and equally American methods of building.

Fig. 127: WAINWRIGHT BUILDING. *St. Louis, Missouri. L. Sullivan. 1890-1891—(Courtesy, The Museum of Modern Art, New York).*

It was made possible by the work of a number of especially competent architects, Richardson, McKim, Mead and White, and Bruce Price. It was only a partial victory at first, however: the great castles continued to be built, often by the same men who had created the shingle style. Price, for instance, built the Château Frontenac at Quebec as a kind of castle in the French manner. Transferred to the midwest, however, where the tendency to imitate the historical styles of Europe was somewhat checked by a vigorous nationalism and where life was a little less formal, the new plan, stripped of historical associations, enjoyed early popularity and in time international importance.

The lofty commercial building was wholly an American invention, brought into existence by the high cost of downtown land (where all business wished to be) and made possible by invention of the elevator, the steel frame and cantilevered walls. By the latter device, still employed, the walls do not carry a load but are held up by the frame and are nothing more than a curtain. By the 1870's the unprecedented height of buildings was posing problems of design. None of the revived styles could be easily imposed on the tall building, though certain Gothic details were possible. Most designers considered the whole building as a column, the ground floor an elaborated heavy-looking base, the topmost two or three stories of lighter and more delicate horizontal forms corresponding to the capital, and the space between as the column itself. The whole sometimes became a pedestal on top of which was placed a pyramid, Greek mausoleum or even a Baroque church, in the hope that some of the high esteem in which these old forms were held would rub off on the business blocks. Such an idea was not new; for almost a century historical styles had been draped around all kinds of buildings housing new uses.

The above was New York's way: Chicago was more venturesome. The fire of 1871 had destroyed the business centre at a time when the city was expanding enormously with the growth of the Prairies. A great need was linked to a sense of local self-sufficiency—midwest isolationism is the outsider's name for it—to produce not only the technical solutions necessary to the erection of skyscrapers but also a new appearance. The man who contributed most to the appearance was Louis Sullivan (1856-1924), whose training and career was a constant revolt against historical style. The WAINWRIGHT BUILDING (Fig. 127) in midwestern St. Louis is transplanted Chicago and characteristic of the latter city. The building is thought of as a cube not as a column, each wall being defined by surfaces with little relief and that little not at all suggestive of any past style. The outside edges of the cube are particularly clean-cut so that its form can be exactly felt as a great container of people housed in identical offices on many floors behind rows of identical windows. On the sides of the great box, the art consisted of careful relations of windows to walls, of smooth surface to sculptured ornament of shallow relief.

The direction in which Sullivan was moving as an artist, and which was to be the general direction a generation later, is seen in the CARSON, PIRIE, SCOTT BUILDING, Chicago, (Fig. 128) designed at the very end of the century. Windows have become larger; walls appear only to mask the face of the steel skeleton supporting the floors; decorative ornament is restricted to a minor role save at the street level where its function was intended to increase the gaiety of the departmental store's display windows. The surface of the building has become an eye-pleasing extension of the interior, formed of the most modern materials by the most modern techniques.

Fig. 128: CARSON, PIRIE, SCOTT BUILDING *(Schlesinger and Meyer Department Store), Chicago. L. Sullivan. 1890-1894. The cornice was added later.—(Photo by Wayne Andrews).*

Although the term skyscraper was already applied to these buildings, the dimension of height was not exaggerated by the artistic device of vertical emphasis. This later development had little to do with the practical utility of the building: Sullivan's lessons in design were good for any height and basic to all modern architecture. The United States had suddenly become a world power in the arts, in that branch wherein its whole character as a country was summed up, the business block in a booming city remote from the traditions of Europe. Within a decade, Chicago was also to produce a new kind of domestic architecture to house the business men. Yet these were only signs, not generally understood even in Chicago and the midwest, and almost ignored along the Atlantic seaboard.

Fig. 129: ARRANGEMENT IN BLACK AND GREY. *(The Artist's Mother). J. A. M. Whistler. Louvre, Paris. 1871. 57½" x 64" —(Courtesy, Bulloz - Art Reference Bureau).*

PAINTING

American painting after the Civil War had none of the isolated and provincial air it had shown in the first half of the century. The public character of its appeal diminished, and the gulf between artist and society, already opened in Europe, was visible in United States as well. Several of America's most famous painters lived abroad as they found Europe more congenial. These people were closest to European developments, as Whistler to the early Impressionist painters, Mary Cassatt to Degas, and Sargent to the Impressionist-stimulated revival of interest in Hals and Velasquez. Whistler's ARRANGEMENT IN BLACK AND GREY (Fig. 129) not only made use of Degas' device of placing a detailed portrait in vicinity to the geometric abstraction of picture frames, but also employed Manet's flattening effects to the figure. Moreover, it contained an allusion to the contemporary fad for things Japanese in the patterns on the drapes and gave to the picture a title that stressed the formal elements rather than the subject of the painting in an exaggerated respect for the art-for-art's sake position.

Painters now trained in Paris more often than before the Civil War, but they still lingered a generation behind Europe. Prior to 1888 when it first appeared as a point of view of American landscape painters, Impressionism had made no headway in the United States. Up to that time American artists had followed the late Corot.

There were also a number of artists almost, if not quite, out of touch with European painting though showing some of the same interests as one might expect of contemporaries. The most important artist of this period is Thomas Eakins of Philadelphia. A European training had sharpened his taste for unsparing, detailed realism, something after the order of Courbet's work of the 1850's. It is not surprising that Eakins was a pioneer of experimental motion-picture making, an expert anatomist and the friend of Philadelphian scientists, for he had great faith in the truth of observation, a fact hardly appreciated by many who sat to him for their portraits. At a time when portraiture was supposed to flatter appearance and indicate sophistication, Eakins' portraits were refused because sitters thought themselves insulted by the homely and worried likenesses that Eakins painted. A great admirer of Rembrandt, Eakins in his life presents a parallel of misunderstanding between artist and public. THE GROSS CLINIC was his NIGHT WATCH (See Book II, Fig. 153), being like the earlier painting a group portrait in which the artist recorded the life of the entire company and its significance to contemporary society not the sum of the individuals who composed it. The noted surgeon is performing an operation described with nerve-wracking ghastliness: in the shadows, Philadelphian doctors are watching. With Rembrandtesque lighting to concentrate attention, Dr. Gross stands commandingly in the middle, between the body upon which he has been operating and the secretary who is taking down the observations the surgeon relays to him. The principal actor, Doctor Gross, seems to radiate power and knowledge upon his audience who remain shadowed by his greatness. This is science at work in an atmosphere of the greatest drama. At the Philadelphia Centennial Exhibition, the work was considered too stark in its detail, and was hung not in the art gallery but in the scientific display.

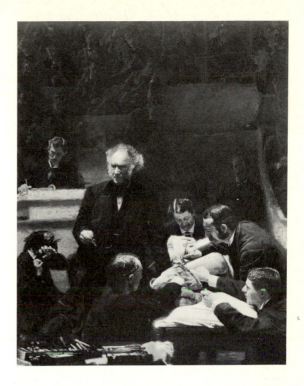

Fig. 130: THE GROSS CLINIC. *T. Eakins. Jefferson Medical College, Philadelphia, Pennsylvania. 1875. 96" x 78"—(Courtesy, Jefferson Medical College of Philadelphia. Photo by Philadelphia Museum of Art).*

Fig. 131: TOILERS OF THE SEA. *A. P. Ryder. Metropolitan Museum of Art, New York. Before 1884. 11½" x 12". Oil on wood.*

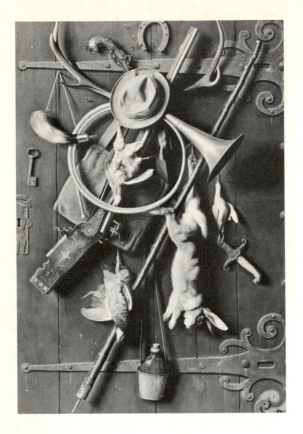

Fig. 132: AFTER THE HUNT. *E. Harnett. Palace of the Legion of Honour, San Francisco. 1855. 70½″ x 47½″—(Courtesy, California Palace of the Legion of Honour).*

Where Thomas Eakins started from a close observation of the exterior world, another American, Albert Ryder (1847-1917), represented a world of complete fantasy. Using such symbols as moonlight, ships on a stormy sea, shadows under cliffs, wind-twisted trees, he filled small canvases with suggestions of strange fears and haunting excitements. The pictures have strong literary-poetic connections—Ryder gave them such titles as *Death On A Pale Horse* or TOILERS OF THE SEA (Fig. 131), and sometimes accompanied them with verse—and this scarey romanticism had certain admirers. At the other end of the range of American painters, was Edward Harnett (1848-1892), a European-trained specialist in still life whose pictures of objects, in AFTER THE HUNT (Fig. 132), or of relics of student life were certain to have a nostalgic appeal to the prosperous owners. These objects, rendered with particular attention to colour and texture in clear studio lighting, were often so painted that they appeared before the plane of the picture defined as a conspicuous surface at the same level as the picture frame itself, a rare seventeenth-century device used to confuse illusion and reality. Both Ryder and Harnett are representative of small groups of American painters whose exact equivalent is not to be found in Europe where the influence of Impressionism was generally overpowering.

The Twentieth Century

ARCHITECTURE

Since 1900, the history of American architecture has been an essential part of that of modern architecture generally: what national character it possesses it owes to the still-important place of the single dwelling and the long-held unique position of New York as a city of skyscrapers.

The determination of the North American to have his own house on its own lot is a gesture of individualism that some communities can no longer afford. The immediate prospect of cities 200 miles across has already channelled new housing developments into more compact housing. America is reluctantly falling in step with Europe, as subdivisions continue to appear while at the same time high-rise apartments are building in town. The single house will continue ·to attract the attention of a few able architects designing for patrons of taste and determined to remain apart, but the result is often a part-time summer house or place of escape, like Philip Johnson's glass-walled, transparent house in Connecticut, the Petit Trianon of the twentieth century.

At the beginning of the century, American architects led the world into a new era of domestic house planning, and their leader was Frank Lloyd Wright. Because Wright's role was international, discussion of the Robie House (Fig. 99), one of his chief monuments, has been assigned to the chapter on Modern architecture. The radical new conceptions of interior

Fig. 133: FALLING WATER, *Bear Run, Pennsylvania.*
F. L. Wright. 1936—(Courtesy, H. Allen Brooks, Dept.
of Fine Art, University of Toronto).

plan and of its relation to exterior setting were transmitted to Europe to mark the first impact of the United States on its culturally more sophisticated parent. Out of this and other currents, grew the International Style of the 1920's and early '30's that invaded America with the coming of many exiled architects such as Gropius and Mies van der Rohe in the later 1930's. Meanwhile, evincing the greatest scorn of European "boxes on stilts", Wright had continued an independent development. The late '20's and '30's witnessed the same isolationism in other fields of American art. Wright's answer to this European invasion is FALLING WATER (Fig. 133), built near Philadelphia in 1936. The smooth surfaces and complete rectangularity of appearance of certain parts of the building constructed of concrete bears superficial resemblance to European houses, though in spirit it is quite different. The site is extraordinary, a rocky glen whose strata and caves are repeated in the house, the core of which is built in rough random ashlar, an intermediate treatment of stone midway between nature and smooth-surfaced cement. The house reaches out from its hillside position to overhang the brook and parallel its course. Balconies provide an immediate approach to nature, of such extent and variety of position as to release the dweller from a sense of confinement to the building. The actual living quarters are more than half concealed behind these balconies and roofs, like a protected cave shelter built in the native stone of the place. Whatever reservations Americans might feel at the sight of the boxlike buildings of Le Corbusier or Gropius, FALLING WATER was the answer expressed in modern terms to the romantic dream of man's communion with nature; as such, it is both intensely American and a basic element in Wright's idea of a home. It is the wilderness equivalent of the Prairie house.

Since the late 1930's, Wright has designed houses, which he called "Usonian", that is satisfactory for modern conditions. Less extravagant settings are more normal. The use of wood and brick, standard or module dimensions, area planning according to inside use, and technical innovations like floor heating, all have popularized Wright's modernism in the hands of imitators.

Although in larger cities the apartment building is now a familiar sight, the models are European or international since it was on these fronts that the problem was first faced.

The tall commercial building was of American invention, however, and all but its latest phases are American. Louis Sullivan in Chicago at the beginning of the century had defined the elongated block in contemporary terms by using modern means of construction to determine his design. In New York, architects still obsessed with the traditional notions of design continued to plaster fronts with Renaissance, Baroque or Gothic details. Only the last, by reason of its attenuated forms, could be stretched to cover many stories. The WOOLWORTH BUILDING (1912) (Fig. 134) was in Gothic style and is almost the only design of the period that does not seem irrelevantly cluttered by unsuitable decorative overlay. The height of the skyscraper had become the only dimension of consequence, a race for the highest being ended by the Empire State building of 1931.

It is possible for one to walk past the Empire State building without being aware of its central tower, which is set back in the middle of a block in accordance with New York's zoning laws. After 1916, these laws had guaranteed a minimum of light, which the competitive builders had denied one another in their race for the sky; but they did nothing to improve the appearance of New York, which visually had approached close to chaos by 1930. It was only when Rockefeller capital and philanthropy was able to assemble enough land for RADIO CITY (Fig. 108) that groups of tall buildings were planned so that they could be seen singly and in combination, and consideration for the civic well-being took a place alongside the advantage to the individual landlord. Radio City has been the precedent for similar schemes in Philadelphia, Pittsburgh and in other large cities.

Fig. 134: WOOLWORTH BUILDING, *New York. C. Gilbert. 1911-1913 — (Photo by Wayne Andrews).*

The buildings of Radio City did not employ the setback method but around them left ground space adequate for light and circulation through raising the buildings straight up in high slab blocks. As an island of order and spaciousness, where the pressure of the New York streets can be removed, such an area cannot return the modern city to a human scale but can make it tolerable. The building, once again visible, is designed as a block with all three dimensions apparent, and its relation to other blocks is again appreciable. In the 1950's, individual skyscrapers were sometimes placed on quite large plots to let them be better seen; or a low block, housing public facilities, is placed asymmetrically at the base of the office block, as in the LEVER BUILDING (Fig. 135), New York. Light and visibility are obtained by a design concept originally put forward by the European architect, Le Corbusier.

Fig. 135: LEVER BUILDING, *New York.*
Skidmore, Owings and Merrill. 1952
—(Photo by Wayne Andrews).

The present design of American skyscrapers has its origins in Europe in projects by Gropius, Le Corbusier and Mies van der Rohe for buildings of cubic, glazed forms, which they designed but did not have opportunity to build in Europe. To the European, the skyscraper was a modern, exciting, and reasonable solution to the overcrowding of cities: to contemporary Americans, it was mainly a source of pride, by reason of its height, to the corporation owning it, and possibly also to the community. A knowledge of these projects, the actual presence in America of these three distinguished architects and some of their works, and also the advantage of the publicity connected with a handsome building have lately improved skyscraper design. Tall buildings have become objects of interest, and not solely by reason of their height. Moreover, they are not the exclusive property of the business world; as

the symbol of modern urban society, they have been erected as city halls as well.

PAINTING

During the last third of the nineteenth century, most American painters had looked to Europe for guidance, though the best artists largely abstained from what was at best a timid imitation. At the turn of the century, there was an abrupt change. A group of young artists noisily declared for an American attitude and American subjects. The country had just become aware of its status as a world power: Americans felt important. It was also the time of dramatic population growth and a wide public interest in the making of the nation by the "melting-pot" process of assimilating millions of immigrants. The artists felt New York to be the symbol of this new America. Taking their themes from the street, parks, and

Fig. 136: WOMEN DRYING THEIR HAIR. *J. Sloan. Addison Gallery of American Art, Phillips Academy, Andover, Mass. c.1910—(Courtesy, Addison Gallery of American Art, Phillips Academy, Andover, Massachusetts).*

sporting-life of the city, and favouring the gayer and less inhibited lower classes as better showing the new vitality, they painted what their critics, giving them the name of the Ash Can school, dismissed as vulgar. WOMEN DRYING THEIR HAIR, by John Sloan (1871-1951) (Fig. 136) is typical. It pictures factory girls of a sunny Sunday morning drying their hair amid the colourful clutter of tenement roofs. Certainly the subject is authentically local, but the diagonal relation of rooftops to picture plane, and the bright tonality of the canvas are both derived from French Impressionist painting.

An "American" attitude had to avail itself of foreign art as well. Most native, perhaps, was the boisterousness of the Ash Can school, expressed in this canvas in the restlessness of the composition filled with diagonals, the caricatured vitality of the figures, the feeling of momentarily arrested movement in the flying laundry. Other paintings of the Ash Can group depict scenes of ice skating in Central Park, New York, the interiors of restaurants and saloons, as well as picnics and prize fights, many of them conceived as commentaries on life in the metropolis.

The Ash Can group was among the founders of Greenwich Village in New York, that neighbourhood whose rundown houses and low rents drew artists to live as did artists in Paris. Their gathering into this community of outcasts temporarily removed them further from American life. In the long run, however, their living in such close quarters concentrated talent, permitted the interchange of ideas, and, being in the city nearest to Europe, provided ultimately the basis of New York's pre-eminence in modern art.

The Ash Can group was not greatly successful, however, in promoting an interest in the American scene: most cultivated Americans thought of art as something too exotic and refined to have such common roots. The group had its continuators, but it was not until the 1930's that the local scene again became a major theme.

Before the First World War, young Americans were returning from Europe enthusiastic for contemporary art, that of Cézanne and the Cubists being preferred to that of the Fauves. The application of geometric analysis of form was easier to learn than the extremely personal pictorial language of the Fauvists and the Expressionists. Though they shared the Futurists' admiration of the machine, of speed and of the big city, only one American painter came in contact with this rather fugitive movement, and he was of Italian ancestry. Joseph Stella (1877-1946) made repeated studies of BROOKLYN BRIDGE (Fig. 137) and the night lighting of Manhattan and Coney Island in an effort to convey the visual excitement of the great city. Mazes of dark lines and angular shapes, shot through with flashes of white, move the eye erratically back and forth and in and out of the depth. Such a painting is almost the record of the artist's experience as he came over the bridge on the railway by night and saw the silhouettes and lights flashing by to confuse his sense of space. The European Futurists were less literal: their fracturing of forms was less obviously observable, and the colours they used more stridently indicative of noise and swift movement.

Fig. 137: BROOKLYN BRIDGE. *Joseph Stella. Newark Museum, New Jersey. 1932. 88¼" x 54"—(Courtesy, The Newark Museum, Newark, New Jersey).*

The European painters who saw beauty in the machine and its products gained their American followers, for example, Charles Sheeler (b. 1883), but quickly the Americans moved away from the near abstraction of their European models. Sheeler's paintings awakened many Americans to the similarity between forms of modern painting and those to be seen in objects where the mechanical function was the decisive factor in their design. When the

Fig. 138: MOUNTAIN TOP. *J. Marin. Museum of Art, Cleveland. c.1940. 16¼″ x 19½″—(Courtesy, The Cleveland Museum of Art. Hinman B. Hurlbut Collection).*

Ford Motor Company gave Sheeler a commission to paint a series based on their Rouge River plant at Detroit, it was apparent that this one branch of modern painting had been acclimatized in the United States.

The landscapes of John Marin (1870-1953) are another example of compromise between European and American art. Following Cézanne, Marin painted landscapes in which the small touches of paint gave both indications of representation—an island or a hill—and by their colour defined the distance by recession from the front plane (Fig. 138). Painted largely in water colour, the white of the paper between the spots of colour gives the brilliance of light and retains as a continuous ground the surface of the painting, flattening out the landscape into a kind of mosaic. Lines of colour shot diagonally across the painting both counter the depth of the landscape, and, joined with the bright colour of the rest of the landscape, express a wild excitement quite unlike the still landscapes of Cézanne. In spirit Marin's landscapes are similar to those of the German expressionists. These comparisons do not mean imitation, however, as Marin was one of the few Americans of the period to assume the attitude of his European contemporaries without seeming to be an imitator of any one of them. No painter, not even the most independent, when he returned to America, ever went to the complete abstractions of Mondrian or Kandinsky.

The contact, often close between Europe and America, which had begun a little before 1910, disturbed American painters, but it produced a mere handful of artists able to maintain and develop the new modern attitude. The local scene as an expansion of the Ash Can group gradually asserted itself again, not in New York alone, however, but also in regional pockets especially in the Middle West. The Depression of the '30's completed a return of interest to America and to isolationism such as had not been known for almost a century. On the eve of the Second World War, the American Scene temporarily held the field. It found its themes in every level of American life, past and present. Some painters glorified the national peculiarities in a determined bid to form a homemade culture; others, because it was the depression, used their art to expose the weaknesses of American life. The illustrative content ran from anecdote to epic, from the social life of the barber shop to John Brown shouting rebellion. In this art, there was no room for abstraction, little for a whole-hearted expressionism that crowded the story out and the artist in. The most famous painting of this era was AMERICAN GOTHIC by Grant Wood (1892-1942) (Fig. 139), painted in Iowa in 1930. It represents a farmer and his wife dressed in their working clothes, the husband holding, like a sceptre, the symbol of his trade. Behind them, their home, a

Fig. 139: AMERICAN GOTHIC. G. Wood. Art Institute, Chicago. 1930. 35" x 25"—(Courtesy, The Art Institute of Chicago. Friends of American Art Collection).

"Gothic" cottage, represented a frontier elegance when built in the 1850's or 60's that now in the 1930's stood for the old-fashioned and conservative. Frontality hardens the composition into immobility. Each detail is clear and hard, unnaturally so in fact, but all the more effective as the symbol of the durability and fixedness of purpose of the American farmer and his mate. When Wood began the painting, he intended it to be an attack on the harshness and cultural limitations of the midwesterner. This quality, however, seemed a positive virtue in the eyes of a large part of the American people; and those who remained indifferent to the cultural significance implied by the picture enjoyed the microscopic realism of Wood's manner evincing a taste for simple, even simplified, fact that had occurred often before in American art.

Fig. 140: LIBERATION. *Ben Shahn. Soby Coll., Connecticut. 1945. 30″ x 39½″—* *(Courtesy, The Museum of Modern Art. Collection, James Thrall Soby).*

The 1930's saw the appearance of much painting sharply critical of the existing social order. The painters as a class belonged to those hit hard by the Depression. At one stage, most of them were being supported by government projects. Of these, Ben Shahn (b. 1898) has been able to rise above anger to combine comment with art, in good times as well as bad, by concentrating on the general human problems, not merely the difficulties particular to the moment. LIBERATION, 1945 (Fig. 140) is a scarecrow dance of children against the background of the shells of houses. The human forms are ghostly flat, the world they inhabit is unreal, and the whole is crazily unstable. LIBERATION is an ironic title particularly in 1945, suggestive both of the feeling of release after the war and of the futility of this feeling. Since a conventional representation of appearance is less effective than expressive exaggeration, the painter-moralists like Shahn are more in step

Fig. 141: No. 1, WHITE AND RED. *Mark Rothko. The Art Gallery of Ontario, Toronto. 1962. 102″ x 90″ —(Courtesy, The Art Gallery of Ontario, Toronto. Gift from the Women's Committee Fund, 1962).*

with European painters who had generally abandoned the simply descriptive manner of the American-Scene painters such as Wood. Consequently, their art remains pertinent down to the 1960's where most of the American-Scene artists are very much ignored.

The Second World War took Americans back to Europe and awoke American painters to a more international outlook. Already the emigration to America of certain European exponents of modernism, among them influential teachers in all fields of art, had nudged the younger Americans away from the localism of the majority in the late 1930's. The whole direction by 1950 was towards complete non-representation. The works of Mondrian and Kandinsky were newly esteemed though the latter's uninhibited display of energy was at first preferred to the disciplined researches of Mondrian. Jackson Pollock (1912-1956) had developed the system of Action Painting when he painted No. 32. For the first time, an American painter was a pioneer in world art and it is under this section that his art is discussed. (Fig. 75).

In the mid-fifties, great canvases (Fig. 141), divided into a few soft edged rectangles of prismatically glowing colour or intense contrast, were the evidence of a more planned but equally intense assault on the senses, executed in colour whereas Pollock's art was essentially linear. The ancestry of this goes back to Mondrian (Fig. 68). But the pulsation of colour, to pursue a comparison, makes it the baroque development from the Dutchman's restraint. Mark Rothko (b. 1903) is the best known of this kind of painter.

By 1960, when the signs of exhaustion of this approach became apparent, public exhibitions of American painters were dominated by these violent and vague images searched out of their own subconscious by the majority of painters. Though the picture-buying public was prepared to follow them, the artists themselves were uneasily aware of the limitations of their power to convey meaning. Already a younger generation of artists had appeared whose Dadaist antics challenged their immediate predecessors. (A discussion of the most recent trends in art begins on page 219.)

Fig. 142: A Rushing Sea of Undergrowth. *E. Carr.*
Vancouver Art Gallery. c.1940. 44" x 27"—(Courtesy,
Vancouver Art Gallery).

Chapter VII

CANADIAN ART

The French Colonial Period

ARCHITECTURE

The principal patron of the arts in New France was the Church. In France the royal government played this role, but in its neglected colony it was its deputy, religion, that supported architecture and the arts by which the churches, hospitals, convents, and seminaries were enriched. At the outset it was the bishop of Quebec, Laval, who gave the arts their start by insisting on the building of sound, stone churches, and who, for their proper furnishing, founded a craft school at Cap Tourment to guarantee a supply of skilled artisans. Among the immigrants to New France, as to all the American colonies, were tradesmen whose training in the old country insured the continuation of traditional French models of the simpler kinds of construction and ornament; and there was the merest trickle of minor sculptors and painters whose arrival kept the colony from falling quite out of touch with European developments. Finally, the priesthood of the missionary orders, educated in France, was accustomed to the use of the arts in the service of the Church and many of them were trained to plan and supervise the erection and embellishment of new buildings.

All the early and larger churches are gone, destroyed by fire or razed to make way for bigger buildings. These were the Basilica at Quebec, whose present structure is a restoration of a building twice destroyed, Notre Dame in Montreal, the Jesuit and Recollet churches in Quebec. Their importance was such, however, that the lesser parish churches reflect these vanished models, which were themselves simplified versions of French churches of the seventeenth century. Ste. Famille (Fig. 144A), the most elaborate of three eighteenth-century churches on the Ile d'Orléans just below Quebec, can stand for the group of pre-Conquest buildings which still survive. It was built between 1743 and 1746, its centre belfry was added in 1843, and its doorway was changed in 1910. In appearance it is very much like a small chapel connected with a seminary or hospital in France. In the homeland such buildings are inconspicuous and little studied, being overshadowed by the great churches of Paris and the larger cities; in New France, however, they still remain the very heart, and physically, the most conspicuous mark, of the villages along the St. Lawrence. At Ste. Famille steep-pitched roofs rise from low stone walls; a wooden belfry situated astride the ridge pole and two towers flanking the façade are the elements of height preserved as a kind of folk preference in northern Europe in the face of Renaissance balance of height and width. The front is decorated with statues in niches, as well as with elaborate windows, round-headed and circular. By comparison with the Jesuit-type façade (Book II, Fig. 85), it is clear that the Canadian is a reduction of this Baroque original, into which the mediaeval wheel window has been inserted. Columns, pilasters, entablatures, pediments and all the other carefully related cut-stone ornament of the model have been virtually eliminated as impossible in the crude materials available; and what is left appears as distinctly separate units spaced as accents upon the flat surface of the front. In the remoter colonies, then, in spite of their genuine desire to follow metropolitan fashions, the lack of resources, material and artists made the sophisticated designs of the Baroque impossible. Not that Ste. Famille is an artistic failure: the designer has fallen back on more elementary principles of organization to obtain a kind of decorated screen before his church.

The interior of Ste. Famille (Fig. 144B), and indeed of all the parish churches, is as sumptuous as the exposed exterior is necessarily plain. Stone was hard to work, but the pine interior could be elaborated with much carving. The nave is short and broad, the choir shallow, the centre and two flanking altars close to the congregation, and the pulpit on the wall of the nave situated in the midst of the seated parishioners. Large windows flood the interior with light that falls with sparkling effect on painted walls and gilded detail. In the choir, the sculptured ornament is especially elaborate, culminating in a canopy over the altar. A sculptured group of the Holy Family is stationed above the altar

Fig. 144A: Ste. Famille. *Ile d'Orléans, P.Q. Exterior begun 1743. Flanking towers, 1807. Central tower, 1843—(Courtesy, Inventaire des Oeuvres d'Art).*

and there are angels beside it. The canopy is of the mid-eighteenth century, the choir walls of the 1830's; the latter are panelled, with low reliefs in the centre of the panels. Over the altar the canopy ribs are shaped in a reverse curve, a favourite architectural device of New France, derived ultimately from St. Peter's altar in Rome by way of a well-known Parisian example. Delicately graceful in proportion, the altar canopy is very rococo in appearance and therefore contemporary with the style of ornamentation of France itself; similarly the apse sheathing is but little out of date. The structure resting on the altar itself, the centre of which is the tabernacle, is simple at Ste. Famille; but in some Quebec churches it was to become an architectural fantasy into which were crammed the whole repertory of Baroque forms. The imitation of styles such as the Baroque and the Rococo, which were already

Fig. 144B: STE. FAMILLE. *Ile d'Orléans, P.Q. Interior. Altarpiece mid-XVIIIth century. Wall and painting decoration beginning XIXth century—(Courtesy, Inventaire des Oeuvres d'Art).*

profuse with decorative detail, produced in the colony a smother of ornament, applied generously even to surfaces on which it would never have been seen in France. To step from the austere exterior of a parish church into its extravagantly decorated interior was to move into another world. Yet to people who lived for the most part in frugal simplicity the splendour of their church was a promise of heavenly glory and a major compensation for the hardship of their lives as colonists.

Old views of Quebec (Fig. 164) reveal a city whose secular architecture was very much like the eighteenth-century streets of Paris and most northern French towns. The proportions were the solid ones of stone buildings of rough stone construction with many small windows, slight ornamentation at the main door, steep gabled roofs with dormers. Official buildings like the Intendant's or the Bishop's palace were few, and unlike churches would never have established a local Quebec manner.

Fig. 145: URSULINE CONVENT, *Quebec.
Late XVIIth century.*

Fig. 146: VILLENEUVE HOUSE. *Charlesbourg,
P.Q. Begun c.1700—(Courtesy, Inventaire des
Oeuvres d'Art).*

The ancient convents and hospitals headed by
that of the Ursulines, Quebec (Fig. 145) have
on the outside that substantial and barren air of
no-nonsense utility which their French counterparts shared, and which was only rarely relaxed
in the ornamentation of the chapel incorporated
within the convent. In the country the farm
house forms followed modes derived from the
homeland. The Seignorial building of the
Villeneuve estate at Charlesbourg is a larger but
hardly more elegant example (Fig. 146). There
was even less adaptation to the North American
environment than was to be found in the northern American colonies where the prevalence of
wood had saved and caused to be developed
techniques which were becoming obsolete in
England.

SCULPTURE

The men who carved the foliations and built
the architectural fantasies upon the altars also
carved figures in the round. Two or three
generations of sculptors in one family were
not uncommon—generations whose sculptured
designs passed from father to son. Statues of
wood ranging up to life size had once been
all painted and gilded after a practice that was
mediaeval in origin. The great majority have
a seventeenth century appearance, though in
fact they may be considerably later. In France

Fig. 147: FRANCE BRINGING
THE FAITH TO THE INDIANS
OF NEW FRANCE. *Frère Luc.
Ursuline Convent, P.Q.
c.1671. 89½″ x 89½″—
(Courtesy, Les Ursulines de
Québec).*

there was very little religious sculpture in the eighteenth century, so that the New World carvers repeated images from a more pious age, losing most of the sophistication of the original in the process. The same can be said of the church architecture of New France; indeed, the type of Ste. Famille had already been established at Quebec at the end of the seventeenth century. Exceptionally, the VIRGIN AND CHILD (Fig. 143) in the Toronto Art Gallery is elegant, even haughty in demeanour, The Virgin, tall and swaying gracefully, reflects the ideal of female beauty of the eighteenth century. If the statue seems crude and unfinished in parts, it should be remembered that its imperfections could have been smoothed away by the coating of plaster before the paint was applied. The competition of imported marble or plaster sculpture ended this native tradition in the nineteenth century.

PAINTING

The history of painting before 1763 is also one of service to religion. Portraits of priests and mothers superior constituted a record of the incumbents of important positions; these portraits were crude and severe. A couple of altarpieces by painter-priests sent out for a short while to Canada (e.g. Frère Luc's FRANCE BRINGING THE FAITH TO THE INDIANS OF NEW FRANCE, c. 1671 (Fig. 147) were not enough to establish a tradition of painted altarpieces. The most interesting objects are ex-votos painted in the fulfilment of vows made by the pious for the answering of prayers for aid. The VOTIVE OF MADAME RIVERIN AND HER CHILDREN, 1703 (Fig. 148), a dedication of the whole family to Ste. Anne, is a naive interpretation of a Baroque composition, Ste. Anne appearing amid lighted clouds above an altar. The drawn curtain is a frequent feature of Baroque portraiture, and

Fig. 148: MME. RIVERIN AND HER FOUR CHILDREN. *Anonymous. Chapelle Commemorative, Ste.-Anne de Beaupré, P.Q. 1703. 18" x 21¼"— (Courtesy, La Basilique de Sainte-Anne de Beaupré).*

the gay, warm colouration is that of the seventeenth century. Under the hand of an untrained painter unfamiliar with the creation of space, the picture is flattened almost to one plane and therefore presents an appearance at the same time a little mediaeval and a little modern. These simple ex-votos are not peculiar to Canada: they are a mark of the fringes of European culture and are found in Latin America as well.

Laval's school had included training in embroidery and metalworking for the proper furnishing of churches; yet from what is preserved, it is apparent that the silversmith got a good share of his trade from merchant and official as well. A craftsman such as François Ranvoyzé followed European models to produce sturdy pieces for church and merchant alike (Fig. 149). In the convents the Sisters laboured with traditional patterns to embroider frontals as densely coated with ornaments as the altar retables that rose above them. No more than the craft of the sculptors, however, were these crafts able to hold their own against the cheap but stylish products of the nineteenth century.

Fig. 149: CHALICE. *François Ranvoyzé. Church at Islet. 1810. 9-7/16" high. Gold— (Courtesy, Inventaire des Oeuvres d'Art).*

Fig. 150: GOVERNMENT HOUSE, *Halifax.*
J. Merrick. 1811-1814—(Courtesy, Nova
Scotia Information Service).

The British Colonial Period

ARCHITECTURE

The English-speaking settlers brought to Canada the customary forms of the English tradition, often adjusted to the New World through use in the American colonies. Whenever the buildings were official structures, such as GOVERNMENT HOUSE, Halifax, (Fig. 150) the hand of English-trained architects can be traced in the simple, solidly built, conventional buildings. These men left monuments to the British Empire; they did little to initiate a lively local imitation.

In the Atlantic provinces settled by New England colonists, the churches and private houses alike were of the clapboard kind familiar in New England; indeed, the resemblance of Canadian Maritime to New England architecture continued to be marked down to the mid-nineteenth century. The city of Montreal had its prosperous colony of merchants whose ties with Great Britain were close and direct. Their warehouses and bank buildings looked very much like those of London or Liverpool. In Ontario after the War of 1812, Kingston, the military headquarters, and Toronto were the chief centres where English-trained architects worked. In the larger Ontario towns,

Scottish stonemasons built commercial blocks and row housing as solid and sober as those of Edinburgh. There was also a filtering across the international border of American-based fashions carried by skilled craftsmen. At NIAGARA-ON-THE-LAKE, the church of ST. ANDREW'S, 1831, (Fig. 151) with its Doric order temple front and small tower, has American counterparts in the Greek revival which was sweeping the United States just when St. Andrew's was being built. At places other than Niagara-on-the-Lake, there is architectural evidence of the proximity of the United States, for example, at Bertie Hall, Fort Erie, at the Moore House, Dundas, and at the Barnum House, Grafton. It was one thing to reject the American political solution, another to cut off a style which was so handsomely exemplified by buildings just across the border.

Fig. 151: ST. ANDREW'S, *Niagara-on-the-Lake,*
Ont. Cooper. 1831—(Courtesy, St. Andrew's
Presbyterian Church).

Fig. 152: OSGOODE HALL *(from the south-west), Toronto. East wing, 1829-32. West wing, 1844-5. Centre, 1857-9. Original plan by Hopkins, Lawford and Nelson. Centre section by F. Cumberland—(Photo by Ontario Dept. of Tourism and Information).*

In Upper Canada the arrival from England of professional architects in the 1830's gave to the capital, Toronto, a series of buildings whose scale and modernity by North American standards were striking. Many were public buildings—Osgoode Hall (begun in 1829) (Fig. 152), the St. Lawrence Market, Old Trinity College, St. James's Anglican Cathedral, and University College—the last two by Cumberland and Storm, the leading firm of the day. With these professionals the age of style sampling had also arrived: Osgoode Hall is Baroque, St. James's Gothic, University College Romanesque.

The history of the building of University College, begun in 1856, is significant of the times. The architects, following the model of

the Oxford Natural History Museum, itself just completed, had decided on Gothic. Universities had first been founded in the Middle Ages, and the two senior English universities could show many examples of Gothic forms. However, the governor of Upper Canada, Sir Edmund Head, was a connoisseur of architecture, and even the author of a book on Italian art. He wanted "Byzantine", by which he may have meant the Italian variation on the Romanesque; then he shifted his preference to a Sienese palace, a print of which he supplied to the architects. Professor Daniel Wilson, who had been an engraver in his youth, contributed some touches of Scottish-castle detail to the compromise which was actually built, a style

Fig. 153: UNIVERSITY COLLEGE, *Toronto. F. W. Cumberland and Storm. Begun 1856—(Courtesy, Dept of Information, University of Toronto).*

best labeled Anglo-Franco-Germanic Romanesque. Cumberland and Storm had dipped into the books of reproductions with which architects' offices were supplied: they may even have consulted the recent publication of the plans of the Smithsonian Institute, Washington, where similar questions about the proper style had arisen. The ultimate choice was hailed as mediaeval enough to satisfy the most studious, sturdy enough to suggest the vigour of the new land, yet truly British by reason of its "Norman" Romanesque detail. Above all, it was not ecclesiastical. Bishop Strachan had just finished Trinity College in Toronto in the Gothic manner, and between

the new provincial University College and this relic of the Family Compact there was no love lost. It was a mark of growing awareness of architectural trends that such a controversy took place—and it resulted in one of the earlier instances of Romanesque imitation on this continent.

The product of this compromise is impressive on its south front (Fig. 153), where a roughly symmetrical plan and elevation served as the setting for parades and ceremonies on the field to the south; it is most mediaeval on the east side, where the classrooms were; and it is most picturesque and least mediaeval on the west, where the living quarters were to be found.

Fig. 154: DUNDURN CASTLE *(from the East), Hamilton, Ont. 1830's.*

In the era before Confederation Upper Canada could show examples of style trends from Europe before these styles had gained a foothold in the United States. The colonial status of Canada forged a close link artistically with England at a time when the United States was isolated by reason of its fondness for the Greek Revival. For example, DUNDURN CASTLE, HAMILTON (Fig. 154), was built in the 1830's for Alan MacNab in the Italian-villa manner probably before any house was built in the same style in the United States. MacNab was not only a pioneer of fashion; in Dundurn Castle he had built the largest house in Canada and fitted it out with the trappings of a great estate, namely, gatehouse, dovecot, cockpit, and elaborate stables.

The usual kind of Gothic to be found, in Canada as in the United States before the late 1840's, is illustrated by the church of Notre Dame, Montreal (Fig. 155). Built between 1824 and 1829, it is the first important example of Gothic Revival in Canada. The architect was an obscure Irishman, O'Donnell, resident in New York. The Gothic is of piecemeal derivation, wherein single windows may have retained the spirit of the original; but larger units like the towers, for instance, are spindly in a most ungothic way. At the time, its promoters justified it to a naïve parish as having a design comparable to that of Notre Dame in Paris and therefore suitably French in spirit.

Actually, O'Donnell had taken most of his detail from English mediaeval precedents. Notre Dame, Montreal, was the first break in the French-Canadian tradition; but Gothic never enjoyed in Quebec province, as it did in Ontario, the reputation of being the proper church architecture. Indeed, it was only as late as the 1850's that Toronto churches lost the air of being merely trimmed with Gothic detail; and this quality never quite disappeared from the tiny churches built before 1900 in rural Ontario.

Another instance of the occasional precociousness of Canadian architecture is the Anglican cathedral at Fredericton (Fig. 156), 1845-1853, built from plans revised in England. Whereas elsewhere in Canada Gothic trim is at the time applied as a thin surface embellishment, the Fredericton church combines structure and ornamentation with the adaptability of the mediaeval model. The result is a miniature but dignified cathedral church on the flat floodplain overlooking the St. John River.

The pre-Confederation phase of Canadian architecture was fittingly ended by the erection of the Parliament buildings at Ottawa (Fig. 157). Begun in 1860, after the design of Thomas Fuller, an English architect, these were inevitably Gothic, like those of the mother of parliaments at Westminster. The Canadian counterpart was laid out on a much more regular plan and according to an elevation having a strictly church architecture. The very isolation of French-Canadian Roman Catholic culture from both the English-speaking population and from France itself protected church architecture until after Confederation. Becoming steadily more florid in appearance, the churches remained as evidences of an isolated pocket of architectural history able either to withstand intrusion or to absorb it. Notre Dame in Montreal might have been built anywhere in North America; but the parish churches of the province, which took over its most distinctive feature, namely, the great three-arched porch are unique to Quebec (Fig. 158). Traditional forms have never entirely disappeared; but the quality of design and workmanship slowly deteriorated through the

Fig. 155: NOTRE DAME, *Montreal. J. O'Donnel. Begun 1823, completed 1843—(Courtesy, Inventaire des Oeuvres d'Art).*

symmetrical front; thus, the Parliament buildings were both less mediaeval in spirit and more like the run of capital buildings. As far as mediaeval forms could be adapted to such an unmediaeval purpose, the Fuller design was effective. But it was no great loss when the centre block burnt in 1916, save only the library, the boldest part of Fuller's design, which was housed in a large circular building patterned after an English chapter house. The main body of the building seemed monotonous by comparison with it.

At the conquest in 1759, there came a temporary lull in building in Quebec. The foreign intrusions, first of English eighteenth-century forms, then of the Gothic revival, and lastly, of Baroque styles, disturbed but did not destroy the well-rooted local preferences in

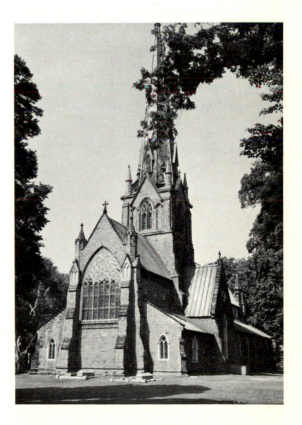

Fig. 156: ANGLICAN CATHEDRAL *(from the East), Fredericton, New Brunswick. Frank Wills. 1845-1853—(Courtesy, New Brunswick Travel Bureau).*

Fig. 157: OLD PARLIAMENT BUILDINGS, *Ottawa. T. Fuller. Begun 1859.*

later nineteenth century, helped on by the loss of a consciousness of the local artistic inheritance. At that, the French-Canadians had clung longer to their past than had any other North American group.

Almost all the attractive architecture which English-speaking Canada can show belongs to the years between the War of 1812 and Confederation; and only a tiny part of it was designed by the sprinkling of architects living in Canada. For private houses in town and country, for business blocks and little country buildings, for churches on back concession lines, masons and carpenters translated the grandeur of Europe and the greater prosperity of the United States into the reality of still undeveloped colonies (Figs. 159, 160, 161, 162). The main proportions of their European models and the basics of European design were maintained; but the elaborations of detail by which styles are most easily recognized were sometimes omitted or through innocence of originals so modified as to lose their resemblance to foreign models. Yet if one doubts the creativeness of this craft tradition, it is only necessary to look at the scroll-sawed eave carvings that are the translations by local carpenters of the elaborate bargeboards of more authentically Gothic cottages.

Fig. 158: ST. BARTHELEMY. *Berthier, Quebec. Victoire Bourgeau. 1866-67—(Courtesy, Inventaire des Oeuvres D'Art).*

Fig. 159: HOUSE—*St. David's, Ontario.*

Fig. 160: STORES—*Grafton, Ontario.*

Fig. 161: HOUSE—*Picton, Ontario.*

Fig. 162: HOUSE—*Whitby, Ontario.*

These examples of minor architecture are arranged chronologically according to the sequence of changes in styles within the province of Ontario before Confederation. They can be matched by buildings of a similar character in most southern Ontario communities.

(All above photographs by Page Toles—Toronto)

Fig. 163: A VIEW OF THE RIVER LA PUCE. *T. Davies. National Gallery of Canada, Ottawa. c.1789. Watercolour — (Courtesy, The National Gallery of Canada, Ottawa).*

PAINTING

The conquest of Canada coincided with the growth of English interest in landscape. The real travellers and their arm-chair imitators relished the record of distant places, especially when the scenery was strange and wild. Accordingly, Canada was for them a rich hunting ground. Sketches made on the spot in pencil and in water colour were worked up as elaborate water colours that often were printed in sets or bound as books for general sale. British officers, taught to record the terrain over which they might conduct military operations, were the first topographical painters in Canada. Thomas Davies (c. 1737-1812), who spent over half a century in military service in all parts of the British Empire—at Quebec in 1759, at Halifax in the 1770's, and again at Quebec between 1786 and 1790—is the most original among them. A leaf-by-leaf painter with a strong sense of the value of flat design in painting, he was the first to essay the colourful effects of Canadian autumn foliage; accordingly, he has often been compared with another amateur, Rousseau (le Douanier). Unlike the forests and streams of most early topographers, his form a strange and exciting wilderness wholly unlike anything to be seen in Europe (Fig. 163). The most conventional approach is illustrated by George Heriot, who had army training, but who was a civil servant in Canada for many years after the Conquest, and also by Lieutenant-Colonel J. P. Cockburn, stationed in Canada between approximately 1826 and 1836, who had already five illustrated books to his credit before coming to Canada.

The professional topographers were usually even more itinerant than the military. Of the Englishmen and Americans passing through the country to glean characteristic or outstanding sights, a typical representative is Coke

Fig. 164: Château de Québec. *Coke Smyth. Canadiana Coll., Royal Ontario Museum. June 1838. 10⁵⁄₁₆" x 14¼". Pencil drawing over wash—(Courtesy, Canadiana Coll., Royal Ontario Museum, Toronto).*

Smyth, an Englishman who came in 1838. His landscapes were often more exciting than informative, as, for example, that from the Ramparts of the Citadel, Quebec (Fig. 164), a diagonal view down over the city to the basin of the St. Lawrence. Perched hazardously on the cliff's edge, the spectator looks down on the picturesque jumble of roofs. He is given a record of the appearance of the lower city at the same time accurate, detailed and unusual. Smyth's Canada was romantically wild, but so also were his landscapes of Europe and the Middle East—a fact made abundantly plain when he later published his travel books on those regions.

Another Canadian feature, the Indian natives were of interest to Paul Kane (1810-1871), Irish born, but educated in Toronto and matured by travel in Europe. Scientific rather than artistic curiosity took him westward, first to Georgian Bay and later, in 1846, as far as the Rockies in order to study the Indians. On his return he worked up his drawings as a set of oils illustrative of Indian customs and dress; to these he added a number of portraits of outstanding Indians. Kane was at his best when most factual (Fig. 165); however, his American contemporaries, headed by George Catlin, produced in the romantic vein a much more exciting version of the Indian.

149

Fig. 165: FISHING LODGES OF THE CLALUMS. *Paul Kane. Royal Ontario Museum, University of Toronto. c.1849-50. 18½″ x 29¼″—(Courtesy, Royal Ontario Museum, Toronto).*

To foreigners, the inhabitants of Quebec were as interesting as the Indians. Cornelius Krieghoff (1815-1872) was prepared to satisfy their curiosity. Born in Holland and trained at Düsseldorf, Germany, he came to Canada after a stint in the American army, and lived mainly near Montreal and in Quebec city. As a painter, his business was to supply characteristic landscape and habitant genre scenes to American and English visitors to Canada. His paintings were small, portable, and inexpensive, making excellent souvenirs. Dutch painters in the seventeenth, and Venetian painters in the eighteenth century had done the same thing.

Since the demand was brisk, Krieghoff painted numerous replicas and resorted to set formulas to speed up production; accordingly, the best that can be said of much of his work is that it shows good craftsmanship. MERRYMAKING (Fig. 166) 1860, of which four examples are extant, is typical. Characteristically, it is winter —to visitors, the Canadian season par excellence —and around and within the inn buzz quaintly dressed French-Canadians behaving with the uninhibited vigour which respectable people could not themselves display in the Victorian era but which they enjoyed in art. The caricature of life which Krieghoff portrayed was

Fig. 166: MERRYMAKING (*Jolifou Inn*). *C. Krieghoff. Beaverbrook Art Gallery, Fredericton, N.B. 1860. 34½" x 48"—(Courtesy, The Beaverbrook Art Gallery).*

for a clientele that revelled equally in Dickens's disreputable lower-class characters: it confirmed them in their own high estimate of themselves. At his best Krieghoff caricatured expertly, observantly drew his figures and their immediate environment, and paid enough attention to the phenomena of nature in winter to be able to envelop the inn in an atmosphere of clear Quebec cold. A rosy sky, the frosted branches and the varying whites of snow in light and shadow are, although a little simplified, careful observations of the qualities of Canadian winter landscape.

A thoroughly romantic artist, Joseph Légaré (1795-1855), self-taught and living in Quebec, saw his province in an entirely different light.

The pageants of religious festivals, the horrors of a cholera epidemic, the catastrophe of a fire—all these are painted in strong light-and-shadow contrasts which hint at more than they reveal. A LANDSCAPE REPRESENTING A HYPO-THETICAL MONUMENT TO WOLFE (Fig. 167) clearly reveals Légaré's romantic nature and his kinship with his American contemporary, Thomas Cole. The crumbling statue of Wolfe, contemplated amid a setting of complete physical desolation, by one of the native inhabitants of Canada, an Indian warrior, tells the story of the passage of time and the fickleness of fame. Légaré's work reveals a desire for grandeur in his canvases not even hinted at in any other of his fellow Canadian painters.

Fig. 167: LANDSCAPE REPRESENTING A HYPOTHETICAL MONUMENT OF WOLFE. *J. Légaré. Provincial Museum, Quebec. 1840's. 4'4" x 5'9¼" —(Courtesy, Inventaire des Oeuvres d'Art).*

Fig. 168: NEGRESS WITH A PINE-APPLE. *François Beaucourt. McCord National Museum, McGill University, Montreal. 1786. 27½" x 22¼"—(Courtesy, McCord Museum, McGill University, Montreal).*

Fig. 169: Soeur St. Alphonse. *A. Plamandon.*
National Gallery of Canada, Ottawa. 1841.
36" x 28½"—(Courtesy, The National Gallery
of Art, Ottawa).

There had been portraits painted in New France before the Conquest, but they were decidedly inferior. After 1763, the quality improved markedly, especially in Lower Canada as painter after painter benefited from European study. François Beaucourt (1740-1794), who was the son of an artist and was born near Montreal, studied in France and returned to spend the last fourteen years of his life in Montreal. His *Self-Portrait* presents a competent self-analysis. Negress with a Pineapple, 1786 (Fig. 168), also a portrait, is an excuse to lavish on canvas a variety of warm tints in flesh, clothing, beads, and fruit. It is the earliest surviving painting in Canadian art which has no purpose but to give pleasure.

Antoine Plamandon (1804-1895), studied with Légaré, as well as in France, between 1826 and 1830. It was in France that he learned the precise, solid painting of forms which had

been current in France since the French Revolution. Painting for the seignorial class and for the clergy as his main business, he also decorated churches and refurbished old painted altarpieces. The portrait of Soeur Saint-Alphonse, 1841, (Fig. 169) made for her family, would be memorable if only by reason of the imposing and colourful habit that the nun wears. As Plamandon painted it, the habit gives to the girl a dignity beyond her youthful face's power to express. Exceptionally, this portrait is full of feeling: most of his other portraits are decorative patterns of dress with sweetly regular, blank faces above them. He also painted still-life subjects. Plamandon's pupil, Théophile Hamel, was more intent upon his sitter's soul than his costume, and the whole interest lies in the expression, serious, sensitive and rather burdened. His own Self-Portrait (Fig. 170) is an example of Romantic portraiture.

Fig. 170: Self-Portrait. *T. Hamel. Provincial Museum, Quebec. 1842 — (Courtesy, Inventaire des Oeuvres D'Art, Quebec).*

Fig. 171: WOOLSEY FAMILY. *W. Berczy. National Gallery of Canada, Ottawa. 1809. 23¾″ x 34½″—(Courtesy, The National Gallery of Art, Ottawa).*

In Canada there are not a few portraits by anonymous painters, as there have also been in the United States; indeed, the itinerant portraitist was busy everywhere. The English community had had the services of a number of imported painters, for example, Robert Field in Halifax, William von Moll Berczy in Montreal, and Theodore Berthon in Toronto. They all handled European styles with some adeptness, and thereby satisfied their provincial clients. In addition to portrait miniatures, Berczy has left us in the portrait of the WOOLSEY FAMILY (Fig. 171), an informal family group rare in Canadian painting, though common in Europe. Each figure is isolated like a chess piece, being joined to his neighbor in diagonal composition lines and given variety of setting by alternate patterns of light and dark rectangles of background. It is a remarkable document testifying to the urbanity of Montreal society early in the nineteenth century. Berthon's portrait of the three daughters of Chief Justice Beverley Robinson, 1846, (Fig. 172) reflects a later phase. The artificial grace of the ladies' persons is joined to completely expressionless features in the conventional early Victorian portrait. Even had Berthon been a better painter, the portraits would have revealed little individuality; the elegant Victorian lady hid behind a mask of fashion.

Fig. 172: THE DAUGHTERS OF JOHN BEVERLEY ROBINSON. *G. T. Berthon. The Art Gallery of Ontario, Toronto. 1846. 44" x 33"—(Lent to The Art Gallery of Ontario, Toronto, by Mr. and Mrs. J. B. Robinson, 1944).*

The Young Dominion

ARCHITECTURE

The period between Confederation and the turn of the century is a rather bleak one, especially in architecture. It was the same elsewhere until the 1880's; one revival followed another, and there were even mixtures of revivals until H. H. Richardson in the United States broke away from this unfortunate practice. In Toronto, Richardsonian massiveness had a real vogue at the end of the century; this massiveness is apparent in some of the buildings on the university campus and in the former CITY HALL (Fig. 173), begun in 1899 by E. J. Lennox on an even larger scale than that of its obvious model, Richardson's Allegheny County Buildings in Pittsburgh. At the time, Toronto was growing rapidly in importance, and its citizens felt the surging of a powerful destiny to be amply satisfied by Richardson's massive forms.

Fig. 173: FORMER CITY HALL, *Toronto. E. J. Lennox. 1890—(Courtesy, City Clerk's Dept., Toronto).*

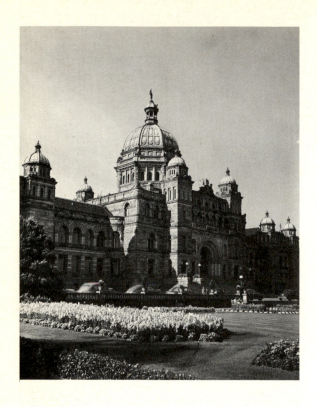

Fig. 174: PARLIAMENT BUILDINGS, *Victoria, B.C. F. M. Rattenbury. 1894 — (British Columbia Government Photograph).*

The various provincial Parliament buildings are with the exception of Quebec's, memorable only for their clumsiness, or, as at Victoria (Fig. 174), for their overburden of ornament. The Canadian Pacific hotels, beginning with the Château Frontenac in 1890, have a recognizable identity like that of a trademark; they have also displayed a grandeur symbolic of Canadian aspiration (Fig. 175). Large private houses remained carefully within respected historical styles, excepting when, as at Casa Loma in Toronto, they reverted to a remarkable fantasy which in more sophisticated circles would have seemed out of place even a half century before. Yet even the mongrel Gothic style of Casa Loma demonstrates by its hugeness of scale and lavish ornament the confidence of the times. English architecture, which since the time of Sir Christopher Wren had been lively and inventive, sank into the doldrums about the turn of the century, leaving stranded Canada, which had depended on the mother country for artistic leadership. Meanwhile, the archi-

tecture of the United States after the bold beginnings of the Chicago school had itself lost momentum after 1910. Not until after World War II were Canadians to see modern architecture of the kind that had first been formulated in Europe almost two generations before.

PAINTING

The first of the permanent galleries, the Montreal Art Association, was founded in 1860; the first society, the Ontario Society of Arts, came into existence in 1872. Their existence signalled an increase of artists in these two centres that henceforth were to share most of the artistic activity. The founding of the Dominion did not bring in its train a national organization, however, until 1880, when the Royal Canadian Academy was established.

Landscape painting continued to have a great hold on the artistic imagination, though it was of a somewhat changed kind from what had been painted before Confederation. The canvases for one thing were larger, the themes

Fig. 176: KAKABEKA FALLS. *L. O'Brien. National Gallery of Canada, Ottawa. 1882. 32½" x 48" — (Courtesy, The National Gallery of Canada, Ottawa).*

Fig. 175: BANFF SPRINGS HOTEL, *Banff, Alberta. W. S. Painter. 1913 —(Photo Canadian Pacific).*

Fig. 177: GRAND RIVER AT DOON. *Homer Watson. National Gallery of Canada, Ottawa. c.1881. 24″ x 36″—(Courtesy, National Gallery of Canada, Ottawa).*

chosen grandiose as if to suggest the great scale of the new country. This approach had been initiated in the United States by the later Hudson River School painters, like Church and Bierstadt, who were moved as were the Canadians by the vastness of the continent with which they were confronted. A. Edson, Lucius O'Brien (Fig. 176) and J. A. Fraser painted in this fashion, the last executing commissions for the Canadian Pacific Railway, itself a symbol of the new and immense country. Mere size of canvas or motif does not make true grandeur, however, and these artists are uniformly better when less pretentious. The best landscapist was Homer Watson (1855-1936) whose early descriptive landscapes of the southern Ontario area around Kitchener express the same warm attachment to domesticated nature that Constable had shown in England at the beginning of the century. THE GRAND RIVER AT DOON, 1880, (Fig. 177) is a typical scene of carefully composed fields, stream and trees, each item of which is interestingly particularized in shape and colour as if after close scrutiny. There is no trace, however, of any desire to explore the subtleties of light. It was as if French Impressionist landscape painting had never existed. Watson came more and more to dramatize his landscapes, by strong colour contrasts, by heavy and coarse application of paint, by the choice of more exciting subjects, as in the FLOOD GATE, 1901, (Fig. 178). Depending as it were on the inner eye of imagination and less on what he saw, he was following a course parallel to that being followed by Ryder at the same time.

Fig. 178: FLOOD GATE. *Homer Watson. National Gallery of Canada, Ottawa. 1900. 32½″ x 46¾″—(Courtesy, The National Gallery of Canada, Ottawa).*

Aside from the landscapes there was little of consequence, and no other kind of painting was to interest Canadians for three generations. Before 1900, although Canadian painters went to France, they seemed to remain oblivious of the great developments of Impressionism, preferring the older Barbizon painters as models. In this conservatism, they were only about a decade behind American painters. Impressionism came first to Montreal in the art of Maurice Cullen (1866-1934), but it took him more than one trip abroad to become aware of a manner of seeing that already was on the wane in France. His OLD HOUSES, MONTREAL (Fig. 179) (c. 1909), exhibits the broken colour method of Impressionism, its preoccupation with light, and its preference for the casual view. What is most characteristic of Cullen, however, is not

what he has borrowed but his interest in "snow lighting". The French Impressionists had toyed with the problem of light on snow, but snow was a rare phenomenon in France and never lasted long save under gloomy skies. Earlier North American artists had settled for a kind of average brightness in winter landscapes; Cullen tried all the effects of day, twilight, and artificial light on city streets, along the St. Lawrence's banks or in the little valleys of streams flowing down into the St. Lawrence. It was more than a decade before Montreal picture buyers showed any interest in his snow scenes.

A second Montreal landscapist of the same era was J. W. Morrice (1865-1924). Going abroad for the first time in 1890, he spent most of his life in France, returning quite regularly until the First World War, and exhibiting in

Fig. 179: OLD HOUSES, MONTREAL. *M. Cullen. Art Association of Montreal. c.1900. 23¼″ x 33½″—(Courtesy, The Montreal Museum of Fine Arts).*

annual Canadian shows. In Paris, he was the friend of Matisse and the acquaintance of the leading English-speaking artists visiting there. If not the most radical of his circle, he was still far ahead of most Canadians. THE FERRY (Fig. 180), c. 1910, is a snow scene but with more structure than Cullen's, the pattern of rectangles of river, wharf, bluff and sky conspicuously related to the frame of the picture and at the same time serving as a composition in depth as well. Like his French contemporaries, the painting is vigorous and sketchy in its application. Morrice's influence as a bridge between modern France and Canada was slight. His art was too subtle for the first "national" school that was coming into existence just as he ceased to send pictures to Canada.

Mention should be made of the most famous Canadian painter of the early twentieth century, Horatio Walker (1858-1938), although his reputation has almost evaporated. His enormous success in the United States can be traced more to his subject matter than to his rather antiquated adherence to the Barbizon School of painting. At a time when rich Americans were discovering the picturesque French Canadian countryside during their summers at Murray Bay, Walker was prepared to sell them pictorial souvenirs, much as had Krieghoff a couple of generations earlier. The happy peasant, his happy livestock and happy, if dilapidated, home carry little conviction to people today as genuine observations (Fig. 181).

Fig. 180: THE FERRY.
J. W. Morrice. National Gallery of Canada, Ottawa.
c.1910. 24″ x 32″—(Courtesy, The National Gallery of Canada, Ottawa).

Fig. 181: OXEN DRINKING.
H. Walker. National Gallery of Canada, Ottawa. 1899.
47½″ x 35½″—(Courtesy, The National Gallery of Canada, Ottawa).

The Nationalist Expression

PAINTING

Montreal, at the end of the nineteenth and for the first dozen years of the twentieth century, produced, if it did not support, the better painters. Its connections with the world outside Canada were more numerous; nevertheless, Toronto was about to replace Montreal as the livelier city. The centre of the English-speaking press of Canada and of the advertising business had enough work to attract artists to Toronto and support them in sufficient numbers to provide the company and competition so invaluable to artistic enterprise. In Toronto they found a small core of writers, college professors and professional people interested to establish a "national" Canadian culture. Among these patrons the most helpful was Dr. J. M. Mac-Callum, whose purse and cottage on Georgian Bay were always at their disposal.

The literary art of Canadian nationalism was already a generation old in the persons of such as Bliss Carman and G. D. Roberts. To English-speaking Canadians, literature had deeper roots than painting in the mother country and in their own sympathies. Sporadically, and since Confederation, with mounting force, serious-minded Canadians had hoped—and still hope—that the geographically and economically disconnected country would find a common bond in things of the spirit. Toronto in the 1910-1930 period was the centre of this hope. Like Chicago a generation earlier, it was big enough to support the arts, was rapidly growing and convinced of its leading role in the development of the mid-continent. Unlike Montreal, it possessed no divided culture of two races and did not have those ties to European taste, which were such a hindering factor to artistic growth along the Atlantic seaboard in Canada as in the United States. Montreal was wealthy, but its millionaires vied with the Wall Street bankers in buying old masters. The collection of Sir William Van Horne, the builder of the Cana-

dian Pacific Railway, was one of the best on the continent.

It was in these circumstances that the Group of Seven came into being. A group of active young artists, most of them employed in commercial art, they worked together from 1913 though they adopted the group name only at the time of their first joint exhibition in 1920. J. E. H. MacDonald (1873-1932) was the oldest, a teacher at the Ontario College of Art. A. Y. Jackson (b. 1882) was a promising young Montrealer who, after three trips to Europe, came to Toronto because it offered a more stimulating atmosphere. Lawren Harris (b. 1885) had been to Europe. Both Arthur Lismer (b. 1885) and Frederick Varley (b. 1881) were Englishmen, and brought the stimulation of this foreign background with them. Finally, Tom Thomson (1877-1917), a native Canadian who was almost entirely self-taught, who never travelled beyond the continent, and who is, therefore, the best illustration of what local circumstances could generate, completed the original company.

From 1912, individual members of this group began visiting Georgian Bay and Algonquin Park to sketch. These were already favourite wilderness resorts of Torontonians who found the taste of hardship and the peace of isolation in little cottages perched among the rocks of the Bay or in canoe trips into the Park. The scrub timber, barren rock, swamps and lakes would not have suited the romantic taste for grandeur in earlier generations. These young painters saw the country as an ancient battleground of natural forces reduced to a scale they could study and paint; they joined in the struggle by going out into it, conquering it, and putting their knowledge of it on canvas. If this description of their attitude sounds a trifle muscular, it reflects, nevertheless, the desire of younger artists, not only in Canada, but also in Europe to live a strenuous life in order to widen their range of experience and to shake off the reputation for effeteness of the late nineteenth century artist.

Fig. 182: WEST WIND. *T. Thomson. The Art Gallery of Ontario, Toronto. 1917. 47″ x 53″—(Collection, The Art Gallery of Ontario, Toronto. Gift of The Canadian Club of Toronto).*

From Impressionist beginnings, as they worked together, their canvases grew bright, the flat pattern more insistent. They were moving along the same line of development as that taken by Van Gogh, Gauguin and modern European artists twenty years before, though with little apparent prompting from these foreign sources. Then the First World War came, dispersing the group temporarily. Tom Thomson, who alone continued the visits to the north, and who had in his being the closest sympathy with the wilderness was drowned in 1917 just as his ability caught up with his intentions. The WEST WIND (Fig. 182), his last and still uncompleted picture, illustrates the aims of himself and his friends. A single battered pine clutching a time-rounded boulder is seen in silhouette bent before a wind ruffling the lake and tumbling the clouds across a stormy sky. Trees silhouetted against the sky were a recurring theme with Thomson, but each time the setting was more simplified, the trees lost some of their gracefulness, and a more solemn note was struck. In his final picture, the tree is the hero of a contest that is always being waged. To a generation that followed it was a heartening symbol of the Canadian ideal of life.

Fig. 183: SEPTEMBER GALE. *A. Lismer. National Gallery of Canada, Ottawa. 1921. 48″ x 64″—(Courtesy, The National Gallery of Canada, Ottawa).*

When, in 1916, MacDonald had exhibited *The Tangled Garden*, there had been some surprise, but from the group's first joint exhibition in 1920 the opposition became noisy and bitter. The war years had created a gap, and the concerted effrontery of the young artists came as a sudden blow to an older generation attempting to return to the status quo of Edwardian days. This opposition grew more violent when the National Gallery of Canada not only continued to buy Group of Seven paintings but even sent them abroad as representative of Canadian art. The battle between the new and old lasted until the early 1930's, the last Group exhibition being in 1931. The publicity had been stimulating; for the first time Canadians in some numbers looked at, and talked about, art. It had been truly a national manifestation.

Fig. 184: STORMY WEATHER. *F. H. Varley. National Gallery of Canada, Ottawa. c.1920. 52″ x 64″—(Courtesy, The National Gallery of Canada, Ottawa).*

The Group of Seven consisted of Jackson, Harris, MacDonald, Lismer, Varley, Frank Carmichael, and Francis Johnston, the last of whom left the Group after the first show. Carmichael was only the first of the converts to this new way of seeing: A. J. Casson, E. Holgate, and L. L. Fitzgerald joined the expanded group, and down through the 1930's its influence could still be clearly traced. Of the founding members, though they saw much of

one another, went on sketching trips together, and exhibited in Group shows, it could be said that they were slowly drawing apart in the later 1920's. Lismer's SEPTEMBER GALE, (Fig. 183), 1921, and Varley's STORMY WEATHER (Fig. 184), c. 1920, both painted from a point in front of Dr. J. M. MacCallum's cottage at Go Home Bay are personal variations on the WEST WIND theme. The first is strenuous almost to the point of caricature; the second on the other

Fig. 185: THE SOLEMN LAND. *J. E. H. MacDonald. National Gallery of Canada, Ottawa. 1921. 48″ x 60″—(Courtesy, The National Gallery of Canada, Ottawa).*

hand is such a sensitive observation of nature itself that it hardly qualifies as a Group picture. Varley, in fact, remained uncommitted to the extremes of the Group; his temperament, rather than style of painting, best fitted him for the ranks of the rebels. MacDonald's canvases tried to capture, in flat splashes of brightest colour, the grandeur of the hills of Algoma (Fig. 185). Harris, the most experimental of the Group, moved steadily towards complete abstraction which he reached in the 1940's. His NORTH SHORE, LAKE SUPERIOR (Fig. 186), 1926, is the last statement on the West Wind theme. The struggle is over, the tree is dead, and nature itself is stilled. Even the lighting is unearthly clear and cold as if the sun had

Fig. 186: NORTH SHORE, LAKE SUPERIOR. *L. Harris. National Gallery of Canada, Ottawa. c.1926. 40″ x 60″—(Courtesy, The National Gallery of Canada, Ottawa).*

no further power to set in motion the cycles of life and death. Obviously, Harris, by 1926, the year this was painted, had gone off on his own. A. Y. Jackson has been the most persistent and prolific of the Group. It had been he who, in work dated 1913, first painted the eroded shapes of Georgian Bay in the way that all members of the Group were to paint them; and it was his *The Red Maple* of 1914 that first displayed the full intensity of colour. After the War, he painted much in Quebec in the hilly country of Charlevoix county. The same eroded land-

scape is there, however; and the weathered and sagging barns and houses speak the same story of endurance as does the pine. His EARLY SPRING, QUEBEC (Fig. 187), 1923, depicts an entirely different country from that idyllic Quebec of Horatio Walker, a land chosen by Jackson because it was a continuing challenge to him. In the 1920's, Jackson began his trips into the Arctic and sub-arctic Canada: he has become the topographer of the Group and continues to explore the margins of a country no longer interested in its own wilderness.

Fig. 187: EARLY SPRING IN QUEBEC. *A. Y. Jackson. The Art Gallery of Ontario, Toronto. 1926. 21″ x 26″—(Collection, The Art Gallery of Ontario, Toronto. Canadian National Exhibition Loan, 1921).*

By long odds, the most original of those related by style to the Group of Seven was Emily Carr (1871-1945). Stimulated by their example but not dependent upon them, she lived far enough from them in Victoria to make her own way. Born in Victoria, a student in San Francisco, London, and France, with spasmodic stints of teaching, she was, until her discovery by Lawren Harris and the Group painters, groping among the varying artistic influences to which her training had exposed her, Fauvism and an interest in primitive art being the most conspicuous. Relieved of her sense of isolation by the Group's recognition, her art matured rapidly in a short period of about twelve years. BLUNDEN HARBOUR (Fig. 189) has the same sharply defined, hard forms and crystal clear atmosphere as Lawren Harris' paintings. Three posts carved as human figures line the wharf and dominate the landscape by their presence. In her early pictures Emily Carr had looked at the totem poles with the eye of

an outsider, as Kane had observed the Indians in the nineteenth century. Now prominently silhouetted in BLUNDEN HARBOUR, their curved forms standing out against the otherwise angular setting, these threatening images are the sole inhabitants of the motionless solemn landscape. They are in balance with nature as had been the bent pine of Thomson's painting. Later her view of nature changed. A RUSHING SEA OF UNDERGROWTH (Fig. 142) describes the dynamics of nature in which the elements of earth, air, sun and water are all involved. The trees whirl upward like inverted tops; the earth pours like a river through the landscape; the sun pulsates; and so obvious and so sweeping are the brush strokes that the energy represented in the painting has its counterpart in the very making of it. Van Gogh's landscapes were verging on this in 1890, and Jackson Pollock's attacks upon his canvas in the late 1940's are a continuation. Emily Carr, more than any member of the Group of Seven, was an artist of international significance.

In Quebec, the "nationalism" of the Group of Seven took root only among English-speaking painters such as A. H. Robinson (Fig. 190) because A. Y. Jackson worked in Quebec. The French-Canadian Clarence Gagnon painting the villages of Quebec translated the houses into gay, coloured patterns and the doings of the habitants into picturesque spectacles. This decorative prettiness was as one-sided a view of Quebec, as Walker's had been.

Fig. 190: MOONLIGHT S. TITE-DES-CAPS. *A. H. Robinson. National Gallery of Canada, Ottawa. 1941. 22″ x 26″—(Courtesy, The National Gallery of Canada, Ottawa).*

Fig. 191: A VIEW FROM AN UPSTAIRS WINDOW, WINTER. *L. L. Fitzgerald. National Gallery of Canada, Ottawa. c.1947. 24" x 18"—(Courtesy, The National Gallery of Canada, Ottawa).*

The Group of Seven was not only an effort at nationalism, it was also an example of isolationism; and its ultimate acceptance, in the 1930's, as a truly Canadian expression cut off the Canadian artist from European artistic developments that were as old as the Cubism of the 1910 period and as recent as the Surrealism of the 1920's and 1930's. One can observe an identical situation in the United States, namely, a desire on the part of the public to clear out of Europe and on the part of artists to find a source of artistic ideas at home. Those who had not followed after the Group of Seven tended to look to the United States in the 1930's. Winnipeg's Lemoyne Fitzgerald (1890-1956) spent a winter in New York in the 1920's and through much of his career sought his subjects in suburban Winnipeg houses. A VIEW FROM AN UPSTAIRS WINDOW, WINTER (Fig. 191), c. 1947, is a contrast between the geometrical volumes of architecture and man-made things, and the organic independence of nature to follow the

free curve. In this case, the composition is enriched by the diagonal, plunging view of Japanese art. The modelling of volumes is precise to the point of ignoring the accidents of light and surface. The American Charles Sheeler was inclined to make the same simplifications from the same kind of commonplace material.

The most difficult Canadian painter to categorize is David Milne (1882-1953) whose life was spent in such retirement that, save for an early Fauvist period as a young man in New York, his development seems entirely independent. Equally at home in oil and watercolour he used or abandoned each medium as his artistic goals changed. In his painting until the late 1920's, he was concerned with flat pattern and its relation to form in depth, and many landscapes were done in a very reduced colour scheme. THE PAINTING HOUSE (Fig. 192) is, in the first place, made of many separate brush strokes in a limited range of colour laid

Fig. 192: THE PAINTING HOUSE. D. Milne. National Gallery of Canada, Ottawa, 1921. 16″ x 16″. Watercolour—(Courtesy, The National Gallery of Canada, Ottawa).

on the white paper in such a way as to establish a surface pattern that at the same time creates the effect of the limited and darker interior of the hut, and the broader, unbounded spaces without. It is an artistic experiment along the lines followed by Seurat and Gauguin at the end of the previous century. The discovery of a theme as peaceful and casual as this marks Milne off from his Canadian contemporaries whose art is strained and self-consciously grand by contrast. In his ultimate manner, his forms, previously kept separate, are allowed to overlap; the forms take on a baroque luxuriance of shape; the colours riot on the page and after a lifetime of ignoring mankind, figures, often fanciful but always human, are introduced into some of his paintings. A winter spent in Toronto was a particularly stimulating change for this recluse.

Contemporary Canada

The Second World War served to break Canadians of North Americanism. The emigration of German architects to the United States in the 1930's had brought in its train an opportunity for architectural students, American and Canadian, to study under masters of the modern movement. The ORTHO-PHARMACEU-TICAL CORPORATION BUILDING in Don Mills by Parkin Associates of 1957 (Fig. 193) has been designed by a man who handles confidently the tradition of the International Style and who studied with Gropius when the latter was professor at Harvard. That it could just as well be placed on a knoll in Connecticut or in Sussex, England, is obvious; but modern architecture is international. Similarly, foreign architects have come to Canada to design the Place Ville-Marie complex in Montreal and the new city hall in Toronto. In British Columbia, there was, even in the 1940's, a willingness to accept the informal designs of modern domestic architecture that had already gained a foothold on the American west coast before the war. Throughout the country, commerce and industry have brought themselves abreast of the times; institutions, notably the churches, have made efforts to rid themselves of exhausted traditions; apartment and some detached housing is up to date. There remains a hard core of house buyers, however, still unable to adjust to the anonymity of a universal modern style, who cherish, as their ideal of a home, buildings vaguely evoking older styles now so diluted as to be too hard to label.

Fig. 193: ORTHO-PHARMACEUTICAL BUILDING, DON MILLS. *John B. Parkin Assoc. 1957.*

The painters and sculptors have become cosmopolitans as well, selling their work abroad to museums and private collectors. There has been a re-orientation to Europe, initiated originally by artists of the province of Quebec, several of whom had benefited by provincial government scholarships to study in France during the 1930's. Toronto, which had been the leader for a generation, has ceded its position to Montreal. The key figure has been Alfred Pellan (1906-........) who had been in Paris from 1926-1940 and who, from 1943-1952, was a teacher in the Montreal School of Fine Arts where his influence was considerable. A Surrealist painter, his work caused instant controversy out of which grew a lively community of those interested in modern art. If at times he has reflected the influence of Picasso, of Miro, or Leger, this is as much as to say that no one who wishes to learn can avoid such powerful figures. In the brightest colours, the inventions of this fertile and humorous artist are the most important link to European Surrealism. The title BOUCHE RIEUSE (1935) (Fig. 194) hints at, if it does not quite reveal, the meaning of the gay canvas, on which the pennant-like patterns are the visible equivalent to laughter. Pellan's Surrealism does not show any dark corners.

Fig. 194: BOUCHE RIEUSE. *A. Pellan. National Gallery of Canada, Ottawa. 1935. 21½" x 18" —(Courtesy, The National Gallery of Canada, Ottawa).*

Fig. 195: SOUS LE VENT DE L'ILE. *P. E. Borduas. National Gallery of Canada, Ottawa. c.1948. 45" x 58"—(Courtesy, The National Gallery of Canada, Ottawa).*

Almost his contemporary was Paul Borduas (1905-1960). After two years in France, 1928-1930, he came back a Surrealist, gaining a local following of young artists. From the late 1940's, he became steadily more abstract in his images. After 1953, he lived in New York and Paris. Large flakes of colour floating in a uniform, coloured space suggest the movement of some form of life (Fig. 195). His most successful pupil has been J. P. Riopelle (1923-........) whose brightly-coloured canvases executed in the main with a pallet knife have much of the appearance of a mosaic set with random tesserae (Plate XVI). Completely non-representational, energetically created, often of monumental scale, his paintings are comparable to the work of Jackson Pollack in the United States (Fig. 75).

Not all painters, even in Montreal, have followed the path to abstraction. Jacques de Tonnancour (1917-........) training in Montreal, has remained relatively independent of the

Fig. 196: BLACK TABLE WITH RUBBER PLANT. *J. de Tonnancour. The Art Gallery of Ontario, Toronto. 1948. 33½" x 45"—(Collection, The Art Gallery of Ontario, Toronto. Gift from the Albert H. Robson Memorial Subscription Fund, 1949).*

174

extreme manifestations of introspective painting (Fig. 196). Montreal had the head start, but since the Second World War there has been throughout Canada a rush of artists to explore in new directions. On the West Coast, B.C. Binning (1909-.......) was one of the first with a Kleelike rendering of harbour scenes (Fig. 197), moving towards total abstraction. A whole colony of British Columbia painters with national reputations are now established in that province (Fig. 198). Lately, a very active group of artists has appeared in Regina; they built originally around K. Lockhead, who has used robot-like forms in deep space to suggest the isolated mechanical nature of the modern world (Fig. 199). In Toronto, The Painters Eleven Group, a very temporary manifestation, signalled the appearance of the non-objective trend. Several were artists who in the 1930's had been associated with representational art. The best known is Harold Town (Fig. 201). As often in the past, young Toronto artists have been more interested in contemporary American painting than in European. In Quebec City, J. P. Lemieux (1906-.......) has discovered, in extremely simplified representational art, forms that stir the imagination with images of loneliness. On the East Coast, A. Colville (1916-.......) paints in a manner pretty much his own. Much occupied though he is with compositional problems and thus concerned with a clear description of volumes, and rhythmic relations, his choice of subject is often mystifyingly simple as if he believed in the artistic possibilities of everything visible (Fig. 202). There are counterparts to his style in the United States. That such an independent artist should appear is possibly to be explained by the isolated and less tensely competitive atmosphere of the Maritimes.

These are but a few names among ten times as many that could be mentioned; and what one can say about them today may be quite out of date within a year. The only certainty is that Canadian artists for some time will think of themselves in terms of an international community, as likely to live in Paris or New York as in Montreal or Toronto, and as susceptible as weather vanes to the winds of artistic change.

Fig. 197: GHOST SHIPS. *B. C. Binning. The Art Gallery of Ontario, Toronto. 1949. 36″ x 17¼″—(Collection, The Art Gallery of Ontario, Toronto. Gift from the Albert H. Robson Memorial Subscription Fund, 1951).*

Fig. 198: MEDIAEVAL TOWN. *J. L. Shadbolt.*
Vancouver Art Gallery. 1957. 39½″ x 59″—
(From the Canadian Collection of the Van-
couver Art Gallery).

Fig. 199: BONSPIEL. *K. Lockhead. Saskatchewan Arts Board,*
Regina. 1954. 12″ x 24″—(Courtesy, Saskatchewan Arts Board).

Fig. 200: PRAIRIE TOWERS. *K. Nakamura. Na-*
tional Gallery of Canada, Ottawa. 1956. 24″
x 48″—(Courtesy, The National Gallery of
Canada, Ottawa).

Fig. 202: Visitors Are Invited to Register. A. Colville. Art Centre, Saskatoon. 1954. 14" x 19"—(Courtesy, Saskatoon Art Centre).

Fig. 201: Tyranny of the Corner. Harold Town. The Art Gallery of Ontario, Toronto. 1962. 81" x 60"—(Courtesy, The Art Gallery of Ontario, Toronto. Purchase 1963).

Fig. 203: Central Black. W. Ronald. Kootz Gallery, New York. 1956. 84" x 65¼" — (Courtesy, Samuel M. Kootz Gallery, New York).

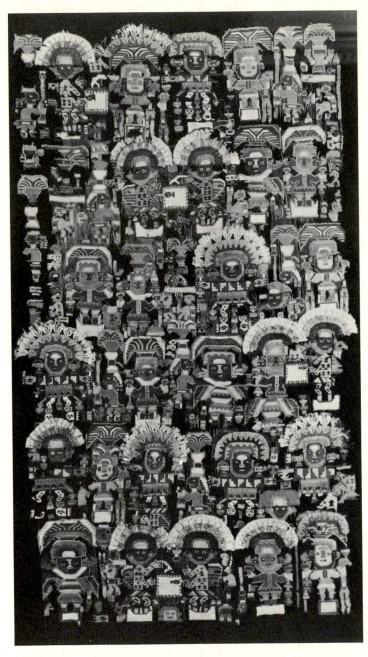

Fig. 204: TAPESTRY PANEL. *Morgan Coll., Museum, Montreal. Nazca culture. Before 500 A.D. 38″ x 22″. Wool and cotton—(Courtesy, The Montreal Museum of Fine Art).*

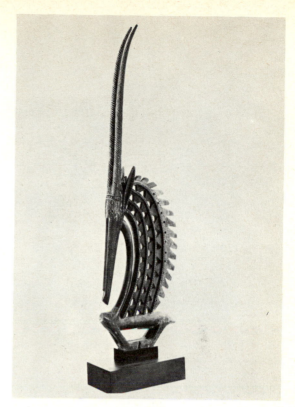

Fig. 205: ANTELOPE MASK *from Bambara, West Africa. Royal Ontario Museum. XIXth century. Wood — (Courtesy, Royal Ontario Museum, Toronto).*

Chapter VIII

THE ARTS OF PRIMITIVE PEOPLES

African and Pacific Art

The first developments of art in prehistoric Europe had some things in common with the arts in their first appearances in other parts of the world. As each society emerges, its art seems to share common purposes and to assume generally similar forms. When European and Asian civilizations continued to grow, their arts took separate paths. It is possible that pre-Columban America would have taken another divergent course if its native culture had not been abruptly terminated. In central and western Africa and in Pacific Oceania, the early stages had not been passed when the Europeanization of these areas began and with it the deterioration of native culture. This is the level called Primitive in art, not to give the implication of crudeness but to indicate its place at the beginning of a cycle of change like that experienced by European art. The primitive phase began at least 10,000 years ago in Europe, and the Australian bushman today is still in that phase.

Save for an isolated group of bronzes and terracotta busts, which may go back to 1100 or 1200 A.D., and a very few pieces brought back by early travellers, the extant examples of African and Oceanic arts are not much more than a century old. The damp tropics have destroyed most of the art of this area, and we have, in a state of preservation, only the latest examples of a long chain of copies made as replacements for those which nature so rapidly removed. How far back these series went we cannot say.

Small village communities living on the soil or harvesting the adjacent sea produced this art, which was religious for the most part in that it was executed to further good relations with the natural forces that affected people's lives, or to preserve the structure of the family, or to indicate the position of the chieftain. The principal art was sculpture, especially in Africa; and in many communities this was men's art, honoured and even occasionally pro-

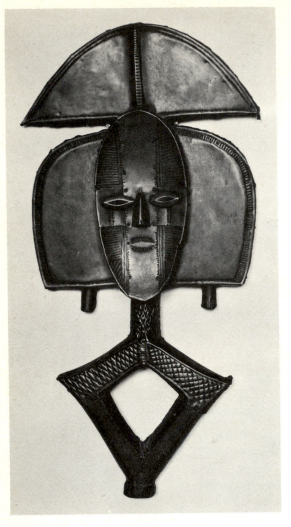

Fig. 206: BAKOTA GUARDIAN FIGURE *from French Equatorial Africa. Royal Ontario Museum. XIXth century. Bronze—(Courtesy, Royal Ontario Museum, Toronto).*

fessional, constituting an important contribution to the group's welfare.

THE BAKOTA GUARDIAN FIGURE (Fig. 206) from French Equatorial Africa once stood over a container of the skulls of a family's ancestors. The statue is of wood covered with brass plates, perhaps to prolong its life but also to enhance its importance. The body of the Guardian is simplified to a diamond-shaped base to harmonize with the geometric stylization of the head. To the maker, the head was most important— it watched—and the design centres attention on the oval face and the staring eyes. The brass plates with their slight convexities and concavities, sharp edges and points give the image a different appearance to other African or Oceanic wooden objects, but this is only a regional variant. In other areas, all figures were made on the same principle, namely, that what was important to the functioning of the image was stressed, what was unimportant, neglected. The dozens of Bakota Guardian Figures, which have survived, look much alike, their efficacy measured not by artistic novelty but by the degree to which they conformed to already traditional models. Parenthetically, this has been a rule of image-making in Buddhist and mediaeval Christian art. Because the powers of such a guardian image were deemed considerable and superhuman, their appearance seems strange, fierce and sometimes frightening.

180

Fig. 207: "NUNNERY," UXMAL, *Mexico. Xth century A.D.—(Courtesy, Peabody Museum, Harvard University).*

Another object with a different purpose is the mask or headpiece, which, when worn in dances, temporarily drew the dancer into the spirit world whose attention he was seeking. The ANTELOPE MASK (Fig. 205) is recognizably the horns, head and neck of the animal, but those who had long familiarity with the antelope and had seen him bounding across the prairie would see, in the springing curves repeated on the neck of the mask, not only what a first glance might reveal, but also the rhythms of the animal's movements. When the dancer wore the headpiece, he imitated the antelope's gait to complete the similarity.

The same method of conceiving the image is found in Oceania as well as in Africa, but the starkly sculptural character of the African with its emphasis on plane and volume is modified by more attention to the surfaces covered with elaborate patterns in low relief or paint.

When these primitive arts first came to the attention of the white man, he was mainly interested to discover, by the theory of parallel developments, what was the early history of man in all societies, particularly, of course, his own. At the turn of the twentieth century, artists, seeking for the elemental in art and for a truth untouched by the then expiring modern European tradition, began studying the primitive arts. It was their use of form derived from African and Oceanic sculpture that has slowly turned public interest to these artifacts. The novel, vigorous, and strongly rhythmic music of the negro peoples was finding acceptance at the same time.

Pre-Columbian Art

CENTRAL AMERICA

A major attraction of pre-Columbian art of the two American continents is the possibility that it developed without contact with the Asia-Europe-Africa land mass on which all separate artistic developments are possibly suspect of contact one with another. If this isolation did exist, the appearance in the Americas of similar forms in all the arts is to be explained as independent invention. Polygenesis, or the beginning in many places, is a very important theory of origins in the natural and social sciences. For American art, it is still far from proved, but the "independents" have the upper hand at present.

The most developed arts were to be found from the Central Mexican plateau through Central America to the Andean mountains of Peru. From simple agricultural communities, these peoples had become societies in which a state religion had great power. When the Spaniards arrived, these communities were further grown into complex feudal states. Chronology is uncertain, but it would seem that the arts flourished from about the beginning of the Christian era to its abrupt termination shortly after 1500. Religion was the driving force sustaining the arts. The works of art are sufficiently similar to permit generalization, though they come from a broad area and were made over a long period of time.

The architecture is large in scale, of massive stone or stone-faced construction, featuring pyramidal mounds topped with temples and great platforms supporting low, blocky buildings. These are assembled along an axis in processional approaches and in courtyards. The interior space of these blocks, covered with corbel vaults, is very limited. Where a more spacious covered space was wanted, a post-and-lintel method was used. It was about the same level of structural sophistication as is to be found in Egyptian architecture. The so-called "NUNNERY", UXMAL (Fig. 207), is a court open at the corners, composed of four blocks. Uxmal was a Mayan city, the "nunnery" dating back to the tenth century A.D. The high platform, reached by steps across its entire face, is a base for a building so solid in appearance that the window openings appear tunneled into the mass. The major decorative emphases are horizontal; and the attic storey, faced with ornament, is like a great lintel pressing down on the smaller storey below. The ornament consists of trapezoidal sets of bands ending in serpents' heads, the latter piled in a kind of totem pole at the corners and repeated in a large symmetrical mask over the doorway at the centre. To the Mayans, the serpent was the symbol of divinity, and they ringed this building about with its protective presence. The design proclaims permanence—and subtlety. There is, for instance, an unusual rhythm of openings to wall space, and a further complication in the relation of the ornament above to these wall openings, the whole achieved in harmony with the static mass of the building.

The sculptured adornment is of high relief in a few planes against a deeply-cut ground, which seen in the bright light is dark shadow. Sculpture was painted as was the case in much early sculpture. Human, animal, and filling forms take on a rectangularity like that of the building. The harshness of the religion has its counterpart in the brutally powerful carving. LINTEL 25 FROM YAXCHILAN (Fig. 208) shows a warrior emerging from the serpent god's jaws to attack a man kneeling to present an offering. The characteristic silhouette convention, found also in Egyptian art, is followed; the space is unreal; the forms are distorted to express their special quality, as in the huge gaping jaws of the snake. The relief abounds in inscriptions, in many elaborate details of dress and other mystifying shapes: it must have been an art accessible only to a limited, learned class. This brutal art seems to have followed a more delicate one in which physical reality was more nearly approximated.

There are fragments of frescoes preserved in Mexico and Central America that decorate the walls of temple and palace interiors with scenes of battle or of religious observances. The conventions of drawing are the same as those of the reliefs: in fact, the relations of painting and sculptural relief are much the same as in Egyptian art. There even exist three painted scrolls, again similar to the forms of manuscript we have preserved from the Nile valley.

Fig. 208: LINTEL 25 from Yaxchilan. British Museum, London. 520 A.D.—(Courtesy, The British Museum).

ANDEAN REGION

The Andean section of this middle American culture is a kind of poor neighbour to the Mexican-Central American area. The mountainous country and drier climate kept the people busy in utilitarian works: their palaces and temples are less magnificent and have much less sculpture. Their most notable accomplishments were in pottery, weaving, and metal working, all arts developing from everyday needs. The Mochica pottery of the first cen-

turies of the Christian era combines brilliance of technical invention with great decorative interest. The yoke neck serves to provide a good handle, is a means of slinging the bottle from a hook, a system of venting the utensil, and forms an attractive part of the design. The bottles are painted with landscapes, with hunters, and with what appear to be deliberately comic scenes described with great vivacity while preserving the primitive silhouette convention.

Fig. 209: MOCHICA HEAD BOTTLE. *Morgan Collection, Museum of Montreal. 500 B.C.-A.D. 800. 12¼″ high—(Courtesy, The Montreal Museum of Fine Arts).*

Sometimes the bottle becomes a major work of sculpture, a kneeling figure, or a portrait head. The portraits (Fig. 209) vary in characterization and are plainly individual, being possibly of leaders in the community. The yoked neck of the vessel is part of the headdress; its shape repeats the firm rounded shapes of the portrait; and, what is the highest test of this art, there is no weakening of either function of the bottle as portrait or as sturdy container by the combination of the two in one.

The very failure of the American Indian to invent the potter's wheel prevented the standardization of shape, which turned European pottery into a mere field for painting. Built carefully by hand, it retained a strong sculptural interest and a greater variety of shapes.

Wool and cotton textiles, marvellously preserved in mummy wrapping in the Peruvian area, are among the world's best (Fig. 204). Employing nearly 200 hues in a variety of weaves, the designers used small repeated patterns on a uniform ground colour. The monotony of the checkerboard effect is avoided by the colour-variation made possible by the wide choice of hues. The patterns are human and animal forms squared to the requirements of the weaving technique. Such extraordinary attainment is not an unusual characteristic of early societies among whom the combination of traditional craft and high purpose has produced unsurpassable results when objects of common use have been elevated to a ceremonial role.

The Indians north of Mexico can show no such achievements; most of them enjoyed only a precarious existence in a nomadic life. Certain mysterious settlements known as the Mound People have left traces of what may have been

184

Fig. 210: TOTEM POLE. *Detail. Royal Ontario Museum. XIXth century — (Courtesy, Royal Ontario Museum, Toronto).*

a migrant Mexican culture. The Navaho and related southwest Indians, having some contact with Mexico, are the only group to show arts of any sophistication before the arrival of the white man. Their jar paintings in geometrical, animal and rarely human forms are like the earliest jars found in China, another possible instance of polygenesis.

Canadian Aborigines

Contacts with Europeans did not invariably sound the death knell of native Indian arts. The Northwest Coast Indians, obtaining metal tools at a time when a sudden burst of creativity is observable in their weaving, were able to carve their totem poles with ease. Animals, birds, and fish, standing for the powers of nature, combine with human forms to tell stories illustrative of contending natural forces (Fig. 210). The narrative is so compressed as to be read with difficulty, the carver maintaining the shape of the post at the expense of clarity. On ceremonial blankets, the opposite process may be observed—the figures are spread out and disjointed to fill the broad space. Unlike African and Oceanic art, Northwest Coast Indian forms are rarely frightening or mysterious. Their function was not to further men's dealings with the powers of nature, but, like heraldic devices, were signs of family importance. The much simplified animals are also similar to those found on the shields of knights. There is a disquieting similarity between the symmetrical, flattened masks on the Indian wooden boxes and blankets and those on Chou bronzes in China. Perhaps it is a similarity born of a like process of reducing animal forms representing at their outset quite different creatures. Perhaps it is a sign of an ancient invasion of Chinese forms carried around the North Pacific.

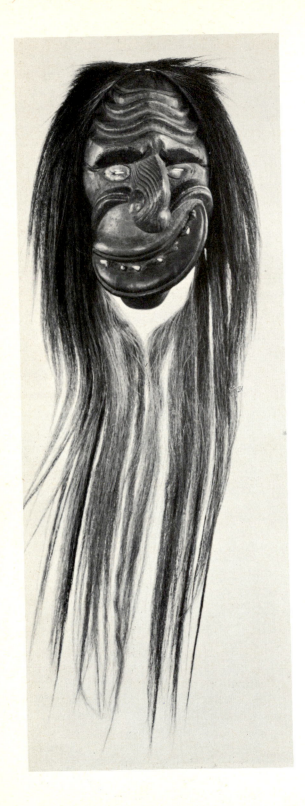

Fig. 211: IROQUOIS MASK. *Royal Ontario Museum. XIXth century. 12¾" x 7½". Painted poplar wood with brass eye-plaques and deer teeth; trimmed with horse-mane— (Courtesy, Royal Ontario Museum, Toronto).*

Fig. 212: HUNTER. *Peter Mathusie. The Art Gallery of Ontario, Toronto. Approx. 1958. 16¼" high—(Collection, The Art Gallery of Ontario, Toronto. Gift from the Fund of the T. Eaton Co. Ltd. for Canadian Works of Art, 1958).*

Another situation is represented by the Iroquois Indians, who, when they were confined on reservations in the nineteenth century, made a strenuous effort to retain their tribal customs. Out of this desire came the painted wooden masks worn to simulate mythical personages of Iroquois legend (Fig. 211). In the short history of these masks, there was not time to develop, either the rigid types found in other primitive societies or the extremes of stylization by means of simplification of planes. They are closer to European caricature: the characterizations they are supposed to suggest are easier to grasp than is most primitive people's imagery.

The sudden appearance of a modern Eskimo art is another instance in North America of art prompted by contact with the white man's civilization. It was the single-handed effort of a young trained artist in 1949 who set it in motion by providing tools and a market. The Eskimos had already carved and engraved in ivory objects of small dimension. Now, using a soft soapstone and modern files they produce a larger and more compact kind of sculpture, descriptive of their daily activities and the wild life they know. The knowledge gained by a constant struggle with their environment the Eskimos turned to the end of making their lives endurable by the sale of these artifacts. It has become evident in the last few years, however, that promoted to an industrial level, the carvings diminish in quality as the artists concentrates on carving quantities of objects, and ceases to live the life he describes in his art.

The sculpture of a HUNTER (Fig. 212) is an example with a double appeal today. It is still a 'primitive' art to the study of which much attention has been directed for half a century; and the massive stone forms are like those of a whole group of modern sculptors, the best known of whom is Henry Moore. The thorough knowledge of the movement and volume of the body of the hunter is not surprising, however, if it is recalled that the European cave paintings and sculpture were also marked by the same quality.

Fig. 213: MAN CARRIED TO THE MOON. *Mungituk. The Art Gallery of Ontario, Toronto. 1959. 19″ x 15″. Stone Block—(Collection, The Art Gallery of Ontario, Toronto. Gift from the McLean Foundation, 1960).*

Since 1959 the Eskimos have been working in various printing processes. Here their expression of the spirit world of their religious beliefs can find an outlet in very animated patterns, as, for example, Mungitok, MAN CARRIED TO THE MOON (Fig. 213). Where the sculpture in its compactness suggests the Eskimo braced and prepared against the physical onslaughts of a rigorous environment the prints describe a release on paper of their confined existence. The most typical view used by the designer is a primitive stylization as is compositional system growing out from a centre without any reliance on the support of the rectangle of the paper itself.

Fig. 214: Sudden Showers at Shono. *Hiroshige. c.1834. 9½″ x 14″. From a set of 53 topographic views. Coloured woodcut—(Courtesy, The Nelson-Atkins Gallery, Kansas City, Missouri. Nelson Fund).*

Fig. 215: SIVA DANCING. *Government Museum, Madras, India. XIIIth century. 3'11". Bronze— (Courtesy, Government Museum, Madras).*

Chapter IX

ART OF EASTERN ASIA

India

The art of Eastern Asia has two major divisions, Indian and Chinese, and from them branch local schools, the most nearly independent of which is that of Japan. In the third century A.D., the Buddhist religion provided the connecting link between China and India, between India and South-East Asia, and between China and Japan. What unity Asian art possesses is largely due to this religious force.

The first important accomplishments of Indian art seem to have been guided by contact with Persian architecture and a debased Hellenistic art practised in those kingdoms founded by Alexander the Great's generals in what is now Afghanistan.

Indian architecture, except when it is Islamic and Persian in source is primitive in the sense that it is architecture without a developed interior. When, for examples, temples are cut from single large boulders or carved out of the sides of hills they are not thought of structurally: they are really sculptured and appear to have a solid core. The later the temple the more complex is its scheme. From the simple round mound with a wall around it of Sanchi (Fig. 216) II century B.C. to the elaborate enclosure of Angkor Wat (Fig. 217) raising its many towers into the sky there is a process of elaboration, but it is of exteriors not interior space. The temple reached its final stage not under

Fig. 216: STUPA 1. *Sanchi,
India. 70-25 B.C. c.56'
high—(Courtesy, Govern-
ment of India Tourist
Office).*

Fig. 217: ANKOR WAT. *Cambodia. XIIth century—(Courtesy, Permanent Mission
of Cambodia to the United Nations).*

Fig. 218: TEMPLE, *Kharajuraho, India. Xth century—(Courtesy, Government of India Tourist Office).*

Buddhism but under the pre-Buddhist religion of Hinduism, which after being submerged from the fourth century B.C. had by the eighth century A.D. reasserted itself as India's religion. The temple at Kharajuraho (Fig. 218) of about 1000 A.D. is preceded by a covered porch in which the various functions of the god are displayed. The interior proper, a windowless and gloomy room, held the statue of the god. Over this room rose a cover that in late examples such as this amounted to a massive and loft pyramid. The Hindu temple interior was an image of a cave in the world mountain, the sacred mountain being the Hindu equivalent of the Christian heaven. The mountain was the dwelling place of the gods whose images appear emerging from recesses in the mountain's four faces for the benefit of the worshipper whose duty it was to walk round the great mass studying the significance of the innumerable sculptured reliefs. In general, the plan and elevations of Hindu temples seem to be expanding outward and upward from a solid core. The entire surface is animated by numerous broken curves and bulging mouldings and an immense amount of highly dynamic figure carvings.

The earliest Buddhist sculpture is narrative relief decorating the gateways to shrines with scenes from the life of Buddha. Buddhism was at least six centuries old before the image of Buddha himself was made as a guide to the believer's worship. The seated Buddha of the fifth or sixth century is completely symmetrical of body, rounded of limb, and gently curving in every contour line and silhouette (Fig. 220). This exceeding regularity is joined to an appearance of soft fleshiness. Unlike the Greek ideal of human form, there is no emphasis of skeleton or muscle, the machinery of action and support. In its place, are stressed grace and dexterity, movement rather than strength, the dancer rather than the athlete. Seated, the Buddha exhibits a controlled alertness, his hands moving gracefully as he teaches.

Later Indian sculpture became increasingly dynamic as Hinduism replaced Buddhism, and Hindu gods, the deified forces of nature, were represented.

Siva, as Lord of the Dance, (Fig. 215), a small bronze of the fourteenth century, is a personification of the perpetual sequence of life and death. His six arms, holding the signs of

his several powers as god, describe an unending sequence of movements in space in which his body, arms and legs, hands and feet join in the same flowing rhythm. The circle of flame by reason of the contrast of its single plane defines the spatial complexity of this movement. Such images are no more monstrous than the winged angels familiar enough in the West. The body of Siva, as that of Buddha, is softly fleshy, gracefully curved and completely controlled in its motions.

Indian painting preserved in the frescoes of cave temples suggests a quality at which the damaged remains only hint. The finest are to be found at Ajanta (Fig. 220). Though their appearance adds little to our knowledge of Indian art, the paintings display the same ideal of sensuous physical beauty that can be found in Indian sculpture. Though there is a little shadowing used for the sake of suggesting volume, it is emphatically an art of contours described in flowing curved lines.

Fig. 219: SEATED BUDDHA PREACHING. *Archaeological Museum, Sarnath, India. 320-600 A.D. 5'3" high. Stone—(Courtesy, Government of India Tourist Office).*

Fig. 220: BODHISATTVA, *detail of fresco. Cave no. 1, Ajanta, India. 320-600A.D.—(Courtesy, Government of India Tourist Office).*

Fig. 221: RITUAL VESSEL, "YU" TYPE. *Minneapolis Institute of Arts. Yin or early Chou. 8⅜" x 7⅝". Bronze — (Courtesy, The Minneapolis Institute of Arts. Bequest of Alfred F. Pillsbury).*

China

China, and its artistic dependencies, possesses a place in the history of art hardly equalled even by the West. For over three millennia, it produced objects of the highest quality, and through a large part of this long period a considerable section of its people admired and collected examples of its own artistic patrimony. Books on art and artists were written in China long before such treatises are to be found in the West, and the essential place of art in life was constantly stressed by rulers, scholars, and soldiers alike. Nowhere have the visual arts enjoyed a higher status.

The earliest evidences are cast bronze vessels to contain food for ceremonial religious use. Made as early as about 1500 B.C. in the Shang era, they are already as technically elaborate as anything ever cast in bronze (Fig. 221). Their ornament consists of almost unrecognizable abstracted animal, bird, cloud, and fire forms, the product of a process of stylizations going

much further back into pre-history. The casting is sharp and protruding. Each turn of the embellishment strongly suggests vigorous motion, reminding the user of the natural forces the pattern represents. Their appearance is not unlike European barbaric ornament, which has the same purpose and may have the same Asian source.

The next major change corresponds to a political unification of China by the Han Dynasty in 206 B.C. What has survived of this brilliant period has come from tombs where the inner walls were engraved, cast, or painted with scenes of daily life. The principle art must have been that of painting. In the Boston Museum of Fine Arts, one can see, depicted in colour on a white ground of painted tile, a frieze of gentlemen in polite conversation, their gestures and carriage expressing the most refined manners (Fig. 222). They move with perfect freedom in the shallow frieze. The

Fig. 222: Painted Tile. *Museum of Fine Arts, Boston. Han Period. 200 B.C.-200 A.D.—(Courtesy, Museum of Fine Arts, Boston).*

drawing has been made with the brisk strokes of a brush, the lines swelling and thinning to describe volume with unhesitating, uncorrected certainty. During its entire history, Chinese painting bears the stamp of rapid execution. In the faces and garments, stylizations of drawing impart a briskness that in other Han stone engravings and pressed tiles mounts to violence in battles and hunting scenes. Like Egyptian art, most of the figures are in characteristic profile and in one depth of space; however, there are indications of geometric perspective, the turning of bodies from the silhouette and faint traces of landscape.

Beginning in the Han period and continuing for centuries, numerous clay figurines, the sculptured equivalents to the paintings, were placed in tombs (Fig. 223). Graceful gentlefolk, sturdy warriors, spirited horses, and stolid oxen from a few inches in height to almost half lifesize have been modelled with little detailed naturalism but with much vitality.

It was during the Han period that the Chinese adopted the moral precepts of Confucius. Confucianism incorporated art into its educational theory, according it a lofty position in the well-rounded life. The moderation, which it advocated, gradually reduced violence of actions and tempered the sensuous appearance of things. Respect for ancestors ensured a slow development of art and a conservative respect for old themes. To counterbalance this, the intense feeling for nature, later to be expressed in innumerable landscapes, received much of its support from another philosophical system, Taoism, which had its rise at the same time. Stressing the necessity of the closest contact with nature as the only method of attaining the private goal of happiness, it compensated for the conservatism of the Confucian code.

Buddhism, arriving in the chaotic period that followed Han, had its great flowering through the period of the T'ang dynasty (618-906). The architecture must have been magnificent, but only a few pagodas and painted representations remain. Chinese and the related Japanese wooden architecture constitute the most elaborate and grandiose employment of that medium in art (Fig. 224). Large wood-columned halls were covered with elaborately-eaved tile roofs held up by complicated structural members. Though brick and stone were used, especially for pagodas, the forms of wooden structures were often retained in the other materials. Set in rectangular courtyards with colonnades open-

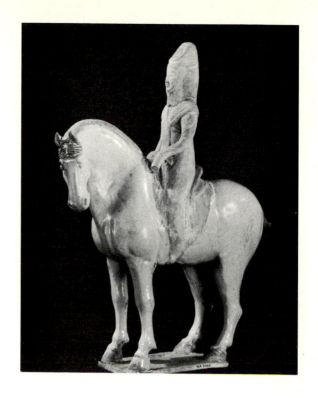

Fig. 223: LADY RIDING A HORSE. *Royal Ontario Museum. T'ang period. Terracotta — (Courtesy, Royal Ontario Museum, Toronto).*

Fig. 224: BANQUETING HALL, *Imperial Palace, Peking. c.1700—(Photo by Osvald Siren).*

Fig. 225: TACHIBANA SHRINE. *Horyu-ji Temple, Japan. VIIth century. Central figure approximately 1' high. Bronze —* (*Photo by Benrido Co. Ltd., Japan*).

ing on further courtyards reached by grand flights of stairs, the relation of buildings, terraces, gardens and the landscape beyond became more elaborate than the structures themselves. To an extraordinary degree, and far beyond that attempted by Western man, these complexes united man and nature in religious or courtly ceremonial.

The introduction of Buddhism to China was followed by Buddhist images transmitted from India to China across the Himalayas. In the process of transmission, the models were modified to more abstract forms. The TACHIBANA SHRINE AT HORYU-JI, JAPAN, (Fig. 225), is a miniature of many destroyed Chinese Buddhas, lost in a persecution of the ninth century. Craftsmen from the mainland had come to Japan shortly after the introduction of Buddhism and their carefully preserved images give us some idea of Chinese-Buddhist art. The fleshiness of Indian Buddhas is gone, the face of the Buddha expressionless and remote; he is a heavenly deity rather than a perfect man.

The supernatural concerns of Buddhist art

slowed the development of a nature art, but, after Buddhism had come to terms with the ancient nature worship, landscape took an immense leap forward in the Sung period (960-1297). The scroll form of painting had already been used for both narrative (Fig. 226) and landscape, giving to the latter the character of a journey by the observer through the countryside unrolling before his eyes as he turned the scroll. Other paintings were rectangular in form or shaped like a fan; these were kept in albums or mounted on silk brocade to be shown upon a wall. None of these paintings were displayed for any length of time: the scroll only as the eye moved along the narrative or wandered in the landscape, the album as leaves were turned, or the wall pictures when the owner and a favoured guest sat down to admire them. Such paintings were not allowed to degenerate into a part of the wall ornament.

BARE WILLOWS AND DISTANT MOUNTAINS (Fig. 227) by a great master, Ma Yüan, is a fan-shaped album picture. The title is poetically

Fig. 226: ADMONITIONS OF THE INSTRUCTORS TO THE COURT LADIES. *Family Group
detail. Ku K'ai-Chih. British Museum, London. c.350-400 A.D. Complete scroll.
9¾" high x 130½" long. Painting on silk— (Courtesy, The British Museum).*

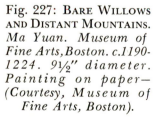

Fig. 227: BARE WILLOWS
AND DISTANT MOUNTAINS.
*Ma Yuan. Museum of
Fine Arts, Boston. c.1190-
1224. 9½" diameter.
Painting on paper—
(Courtesy, Museum of
Fine Arts, Boston).*

Fig. 228: SIX PERSIMMONS. *Mu Ch'i. Ryukoin Temple, Kyoto, Japan. XIIIth century. 14" x 15". Ink on paper—(Photo by Benrido Co. Ltd., Japan).*

exist as if they were real and not painted. The blue haze and the white path arouse a longing to walk in them." Again, "The spring mountain is wrapped in an unbroken stretch of dreamy haze and mist, and the men are joyful; the summer mountain is rich with shady foliage and the men are peaceful; the autumn mountain is sere and calm, with leaves falling and men are solemn; the winter mountain is heavy with storm clouds and withdrawn, and men are forlorn." Man and nature are in harmony. It will be noticed that even in winter there is no excess of unhappiness, just a gentle melancholy.

Fig. 229: WINTER LANDSCAPE. *Sesshu. Manjuin Temple, Kyoto, Japan. Late XVth century. 18" x 12". Ink on paper—(Photo by Benrido Co. Ltd., Japan).*

evocative of the mood of man in winter in face of the emptiness of the landscape. The drooping willow in the right foreground and the dim silhouettes of mountains in the left distance form an axis along which the viewer wanders in imagination, passing a traveller, crossing a bridge, and gaining the hamlet nestled in trees at the lake's edge. The world spreads indefinitely beyond and to the sides of the road; however, unlike Western landscape, infinite extension into the distance is not a major concern. Form is described with a minimum of line, thus leaving much to the viewer's imagination. Shading, as it appears on tree trunk or mountain, produces volume without weight or serves as a token of light. A mist hovering in the valleys and at the base of trees in the forest joins earth to air.

A Chinese painter, writing in the eleventh century, said of landscape paintings, "They

Amongst Europeans, only Rembrandt was as thoroughly at home in the landscape and possessed a drawing skill equal to that of the Chinese. Those Westerners who have approached the Chinese have all been northern Europeans; and however close they have come in their drawings, in their finished paintings they retired, so to speak, outside the frame to look at nature often as through a window to the outdoors.

All European art set alongside Chinese paintings appears tentative and uncertain, the form upon the canvas finally achieved as a discovery. The Chinese painter by contrast practised his art incessantly in order to achieve an automatic facility. His easy flowing ink and delicate silk or paper surfaces allowed of no correction, the fine hair brushes responding to the slightest change of pressure or direction. A theory of the creative act as a spontaneous burst of creation keeping pace with the artist's sudden insight after long meditation was put forward by a branch of Buddhism known as Zen. According to Zen's theory, the creator was not to be hindered by mechanical considerations; if it so moved him he should paint even with his fingers. The brush strokes of

Mu-chi's SIX PERSIMMONS (Fig. 228) can be numbered; they vary from a full load of ink to the faint fleck of a nearly dry brush point. There is nowhere a slight fumbling that may be hidden. If the result may seem slight and bare, the Zen artist would not have been surprised. The SIX PERSIMMONS was meaningful only to those who had prepared themselves by meditation to see, like Mu-chi, in this little cluster of fruit an explanation of the order of all creation. The modern artist often claims a like importance for his work, and shows a similar scorn for those who think his work too simple.

Because he valued the sudden burst of creation after a long preparation the Zen painter's work is often violent in its expression. WINTER LANDSCAPE (Fig. 229) by an important Japanese Zen practitioner Sesshu (1420-1506) who came to China to study, illustrates this quality. The brush strokes are angular and broad, blots are frequent and the whole impression is that of something hurriedly and wildly set down. The total mood of winter as a time of harshness is conveyed to the viewer more by the method of painting than by the indications of the season in the form of bare trees or snow-covered rocks.

Fig. 230: THE BURNING OF THE SANJO PALACE *(detail). Anonymous. Museum of Fine Arts, Boston. XIIIth century. Complete scroll 16" high x 22'11" long. Painting on paper— (Courtesy, Museum of Fine Arts, Boston).*

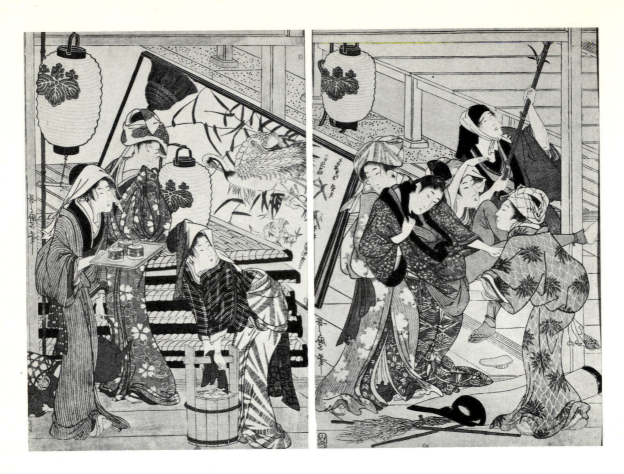

Fig. 231: HOUSE CLEANING AT THE END OF THE YEAR. *Utamaro. c.1800. Coloured woodcut. Two of a series of five plates—(Courtesy, The Nelson-Atkins Gallery, Kansas City, Missouri. Nelson Fund).*

Japan

By the sixteenth century, Chinese art had lost all its power of new invention; conservatism had stopped exploration of new directions. The Japanese, while adopting the traditions of the mainland, preserved a strongly local tinge in their art. The vitality was such that it was still developing new forms when Japan opened its ports to the West in 1853. Until the eleventh century, Japanese art is Chinese art transplanted, but a political crisis separating the two countries produced in short order a native manner called by the Japanese Yamato-e.

Depicting incidents from history, popular religious tradition and fiction, Yamato-e at-

tained its greatest heights in the continuous scroll (Fig. 230). The point of view in most of these scrolls is that of an observer above the scenes, looking down diagonally in the role of an interested eyewitness. When events take place indoors, the roofs of buildings are removed. The drawing is lively. A good deal of local colour is used in most scrolls in areas of flat tone against the neutral background. Each scroll is prodigal of details: crowds are frequent, and always there are interested spectators and minor participants. On the surface of life, the Japanese found ample materials.

In its first phase, Yamato-e included most

levels of society; the lower classes were vulgar caricatures; the upper classes uniformly elegant. As Japanese society separated into rigidly divided strata, the feudal nobility patronized arts of the greatest magnificence. Large six-part folding screens, often painted black on gold-leaf grounds that were made to separate the spaces inside the large feudal palaces.

The common man's art became the woodblock print, enriched by colour printing in the eighteenth century. The technique had been used in China since the eighth century, originally for popular religious images; the emergence of an independent and enterprising urban society in Japan elevated this heretofore humble art. At first, the subjects were portraits of popular entertainers; then, the characteristic activities of city people; and, ultimately, landscape. The traditions of Yamato-e painting repeated in the woodblock print became known in Europe in the mid-nineteenth century. Utamaro's HOUSE CLEANING AT THE END OF THE YEAR (Fig. 231) is a comical print of the idle youth who has become almost a permanent part of the furniture to be moved out of doors like rubbish when the house is to be cleaned. It is a double print, each part itself a unit. The field of vision is that of a person placed

slightly above and to the right of the room, the space of which is laid out in parallel perspective. Walls, floor, screen and mattresses that define the space are cut off by the frame: their fragments suggest the casual position of the viewer. There is simultaneously a composition in depth and a very special emphasis on the flatness of the design in the foreground. The curving silhouettes of the women are filled in with colour to make flat patches intersecting the angular shapes of forms receding into depth. A complete absence of shading within the figures furthers the sense of flat pattern. From Manet, THE FIFER (Fig. 29) to Toulouse-Lautrec, THE CIRCUS FERNANDO (Fig. 44) European painters have left a trail of evidence of borrowing pictorial devices such as these that have been noted here.

In the last phase of the development of the Japanese woodblock landscape views of a topographical nature in long series became popular. Hokusai, THE GREAT WAVE AT KANA (Fig. 232) and Hiroshige, SUDDEN SHOWER AT SHONO (Fig. 214) belong to such series. In the traditional oriental landscape the prints are inhabited by men going about their daily activities, sometimes discomfited temporarily by nature's whims but never threatened by a hostile force.

Fig. 232: GREAT WAVE AT KANA. *Hokusai. 1823-29. 10" x 15". Coloured woodcut — (Courtesy, The Metropolitan Museum of Art, Rogers Fund, 1914).*

Fig. 233: KURO—SHOIN, *interior. Kyoto. Late XVIth century— (Photo by Benrido Co. Ltd., Japan).*

Even when the waves rear up above the boat in the trough of the sea, the little craft's crescent shape merely adds to the swiftness of the movement of the waves. It seems in no danger of swamping. When the crest of the wave breaks in a feather of falling water or the rain comes down in driving sheets, the artists did not aim for anything like the simple physical appearance of natural phenomena. By inventing an equivalent in line they have adhered to oriental landscape tradition and avoided the western attempt to approximate the whole appearance of the visible world.

The interest in the Japanese print had hardly died down at the beginning of the twentieth century when American architects, headed by Frank Lloyd Wright, began to draw on Japanese architecture for new forms.

Chinese influence was very strong on temple architecture in Japan: Buddhism had come from the mainland and its forms accompanied it. In domestic architecture, however, even of palatial scale, a native Japanese feeling intruded and was at times dominant (Fig. 233). This feeling is a studied simplicity created by designers working in native woods, paper, and plaster, often without further embellishment than the natural plain or polished surfaces. With

simplicity went asymmetry of composition. So grouped, the parts of a building could be fitted into the contrived naturalness of surrounding gardens. Transitions from indoors to outdoors in the forms of door openings, screened porches, and removable walls brought the dweller into intimate contact with nature. Within the house, sliding doors and movable screens permitted innumerable modifications on the arrangement of the interior space. The unadorned rectangular panelling of the walls depended for their harmony on a careful ordering of proportions. The essentials of this architecture seem to have been quite perfected by the sixteenth century, and, having spread through all levels of Japanese society, was able to resist foreign infiltration and ultimately to influence the West as well. The Katsura palace, Kyoto, (Fig. 234) is an imperial residence, but it is infinitely closer to the peasant home than Versailles is to the French peasant's cottage.

Many of the characteristics of modern architecture seem to have been anticipated in the Japanese house, for example, the informality of plan, the easy transition from inside to outdoors, the continuity of spaces within. In America, at least, we can assign to Japanese domestic architecture a role comparable in importance to that played by the woodblock print.

Fig. 234: KATSURA PALACE, *Kyoto exterior. XVIIth century— (Photo by Benrido Co. Ltd., Japan).*

Plate I: COMTESSE D'HAUSSONVILLE. J. A. D. Ingres. Frick Collection, New York. 1845. 49⅞" x 35⅝"—(Copyright, The Frick Collection, New York). York.).

Plate II: ABDUCTION OF REBECCA. *E. Delacroix. Metropolitan Museum, New York.*
1846. 39½" x 32½".—(Courtesy, The Metropolitan Museum of Art, Wolfe Fund, 1903).

Plate III. IDEAL LANDSCAPE (MERCURY AND ARGUS). *J. M. W. Turner.*
National Gallery, Ottawa. 1836. 59″ x 43″—(Collection of The National
Gallery of Canada, Ottawa).

Plate IV: SALISBURY CATHEDRAL. *John Constable. Frick Collection, New York. 1826. 34½″ x 43⅝″* —(*Copyright, The Frick Collection, New York*).

Plate V: MISS VAN BUREN. *Thomas Eakins. The Phillips Collection, Washington. c.1891. 54″ x 32″—(Courtesy, The Phillips Collection, Washington).*

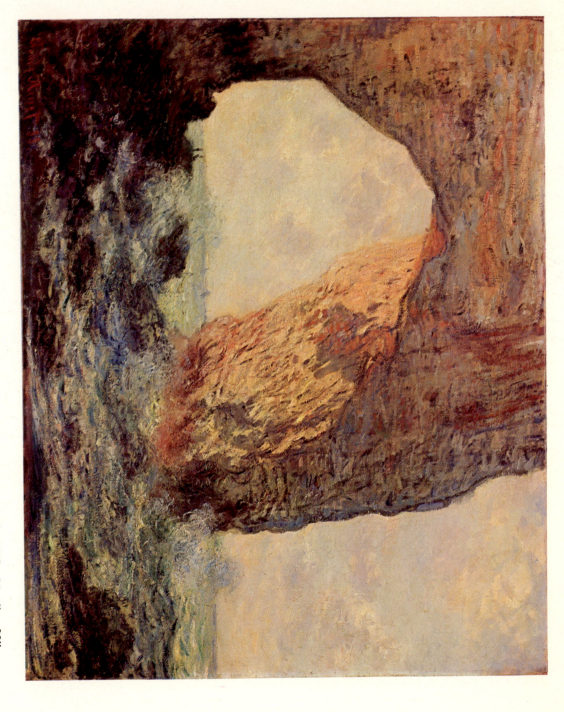

Plate VI: THE CLIFF AT ETRETAT. C. Monet. Metropolitan Museum, New York. 1883. 25¾″ x 32″ —(Courtesy, The Metropolitan Museum of Art, Bequest of William Church Osborn, 1951).

Plate VII: THE YELLOW CHRIST. *P. Gauguin. Albright-Knox Art Gallery, Buffalo. 1889. 36¼" x 28⅞"—(Courtesy, Albright-Knox Art Gallery, Buffalo, New York).*

Plate VIII: Monte Ste. Victoire. P. Cézanne. *The Phillips Collection, Washington.* 1885-1887. 23½" x 28½"—*(Courtesy, The Phillips Collection, Washington).*

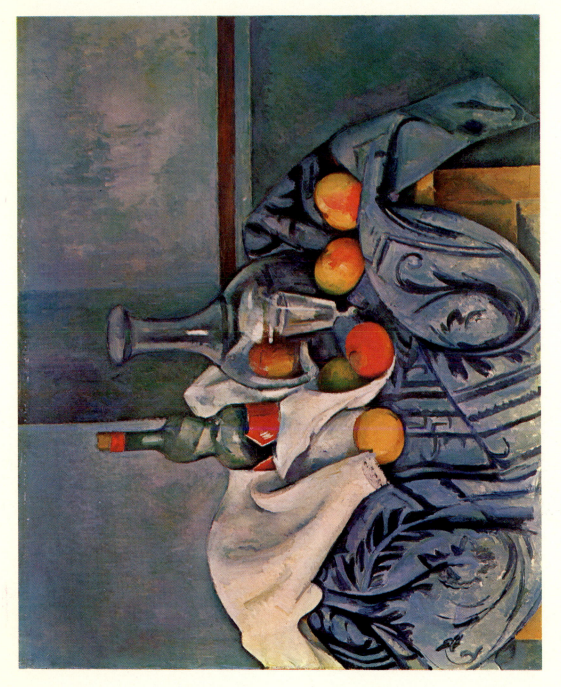

Plate IX: STILL LIFE WITH PEPPERMINT BOTTLE. *P. Cézanne. National Gallery, Washington. 25½" x 31½"—(Courtesy, National Gallery of Art, Washington, D.C., Samuel H. Kress Collection).*

Plate X: A Sunday Afternoon on the Island of La Grande Jatte. G. Seurat. The Art Institute of Chicago. 1884-1886. 81¼″ x 120¼″—(Courtesy, The Art Institute of Chicago).

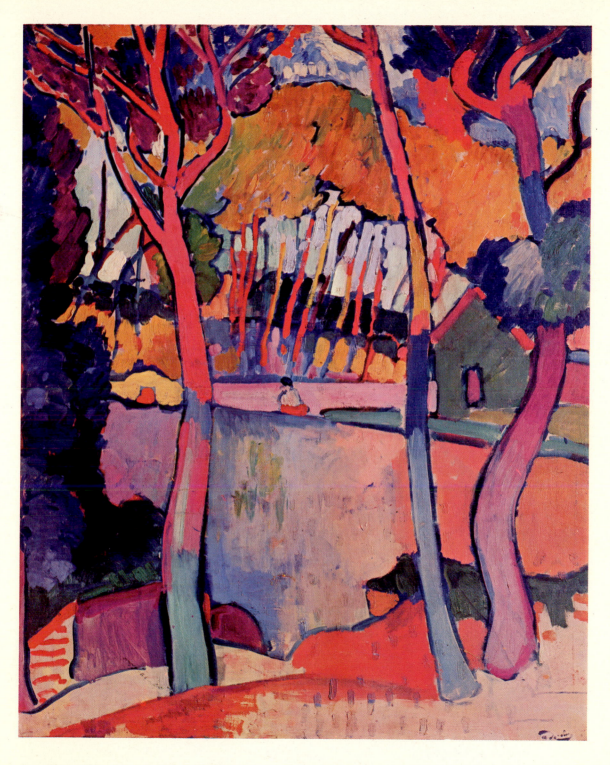

Plate XI: THREE TREES, L'ESTAQUE. *A. Derain. Zacks Collection, Toronto. 1906.*
38″ x 30½″—(Courtesy, Ayala and Sam Zacks, Toronto).

Plate XII: YELLOW SUNSET. *Tom Thomson. National Gallery, Ottawa. c.1916.*
8½″ x 10½″—(Collection of The National Gallery of Canada, Ottawa).

Plate XIII: ORCHIS AND ARUM. D. Milne. The Art Gallery of Ontario, Toronto. 1947. 14″ x 21″. Watercolour—(Collection, The Art Gallery of Ontario. Toronto. Gift from the Fund of the T. Eaton Co. Ltd. for Canadian Works of Art, 1948).

Plate XIV: VIOLIN AND PALETTE. *G. Braque. Guggenheim Museum, New York. 1909-1910. 36¼″ x 16⅞″—(The Solomon R. Guggenheim Museum Collection).*

Plate XV: Composition. *W. Kandinsky. Albright-Knox Art Gallery, Buffalo.*
.1913. 34½″ x 39¼″—(Courtesy, Albright-Knox Art Gallery, Buffalo, New York).

Plate XVI: LA ROUE, No. 2. *J. P. Riopelle. National Gallery, Ottawa. 1957.*
78½″ x 78½″—(Collection of The National Gallery of Canada, Ottawa).

Appendix

RECENT TRENDS IN ART

Pop Art

The search for a contemporary mode of expression led the artists of the early 1960's to draw on objects representative of contemporary culture such as Campbell Soup cans, bathroom fixtures and comic-strip blowups of Superman. New ideas were examined, perhaps fruitfully; for instance, the repetition of a pattern by the photo-lithographic process, and the quality of softness inherent in sculpture. Almost invariably the results have been harsh in their contrasts, brutal in line and loud in colour. Though there is a note of satire in the work of some Pop artists, most adhere to a serious belief that vitality exists only at the level of this popular art. It originated mainly in the United States, and when found elsewhere, bears witness to an admiration of American values.

An example of Pop Art is Robert Indiana's TAKE FIVE (Fig. 235), composed of a repeated pattern of five-piece units. They look like labels or stamps decorated with "commercial art" forms in simple, bold colours. Slogan-like, the words "Eat, Err, Hug, Die" are a sardonic comment on the "American Dream" or on popular philosophy.

Op Art

The crest of Pop Art passed before 1965, to be followed by Op (short for "optical") Art. In this school, non-representative things defined by clean or "hard" edges recalled the Cubist and Bauhaus investigations of form during the 1920's. Changes of pattern caused by a shifting point of view and optical illusions are popular but not found in every instance, and many works have the appearance of illustrations for text books in optics, psychology or geometry.

Environments

As the decade draws to a close, teams of artists are collaborating to create situations in which the senses are bombarded simultaneously with impressions gained from touch, sight, sound and smell. These works or situations are called Environments and as they imply, destroy the traditional separation between man and the work of art. They have three dimensions, of course, but they are almost impossible to define since light and sound and even pulsating surfaces may be involved. Such mass attacks on the senses pose problem in terms of combining the various media toward a unified effect and are still experimental. We might remember that the Gothic cathedrals and what went on in them comprised Environments; though our hindsight makes it easier for us to see what was the unifying purpose in these models.

Fig. 235: THE DEMUTH AMERICAN DREAM NO. 5. *Robert Indiana. The Art Gallery of Ontario, Toronto. 144" x 144" — (Collection, The Art Gallery of Ontario, Toronto. Gift from the Women's Committee Fund, 1964.)*

Glossary

Abstract Art — A conception of art which assumes that there are artistic values in forms and colours without the need of subject.

Action Painting — A form of *Abstract Art* in which the painter introduces as much and as vigorous physical action as possible to cause a spontaneous and uncontrolled distribution of dribbles and splashes on the canvas. This nearly complete release from rational control is, in the opinion of the artists who practise this method, a release from cramping inhibitions.

Analytic Cubism — *see Cubism.*

Aquatint — A variation on the etching process (*see* Etching). The resinous protective surface applied in etching is made porous by a number of means so that the acid bites through many small holes to form an evenly pitted surface on the plate. This prints as cloudy or atmospheric effects. When the desired density of cloud is obtained, that surface is protected by a non-porous resin covering the linear part of the design obtained by the conventional methods. The technique was at its peak of favour in the nineteenth century.

Art Nouveau — A movement which spread through Europe and to America in the 1890's and persisted for a generation. It was mainly an art of decoration in the applied arts and on the surface of buildings. The forms were derived from animal and vegetable shapes, twisted in a semi-abstract curvi-linear manner often almost beyond recognition. It is known in Germany as Jugendstil from its use in a magazine "Jugend".

Archaeology — The study of a vanished civilization through its material remains. In the early days of Archaeology, the search was directed mainly to the discovery of works of art. The beginning of scientific archaeology dated from the last third of the nineteenth century when excavators began to pay attention to less impressive but historically informative remains such as pottery, inscriptions, coins, etc.

Ashlar — Cut stones, usually rectangular, for the facing of walls.

Balloon Construction — A method of framing wood houses which in mid-nineteenth century America made possible a greater freedom of planning than the older method of building.

Bargeboard — The broad facings of eaves of Gothic Revival houses carved in elaborate repeat patterns, based originally on late Gothic ornamental forms but by 1860 becoming quite free and fanciful in their patterns.

Baroque Revival — Architecture borrowing from seventeenth century sources to be found in Europe and America in the mid-nineteenth century. The Baroque Revival was particularly favoured for large public buildings, and palatial private dwellings.

Coloured Woodblock — The process of graphic reproduction whereby several separate woodblocks, each bearing portions of the whole design, are inked in different colours and printed successively one over the other. Though the process was known and sporadically used in Europe, the Japanese perfected the most subtle use of the technique. The areas of colour being flat tend to flatten the whole design. Line as contour was printed black.

Cantilevered Construction — A method of building with steel beams by which the floor beams anchored in the cage of steel formed by the frame carry at each level the weight of the outside wall. Each storey of outer wall weight is the same and there is no need to thicken the base of the wall to support higher storeys. The physical properties of structural steel made possible this new technique which is much more economical of labour than the elaborate masonry necessary in earlier architecture. The very large windows opened in the light stone facing gave more light within. Eventually it became possible to use window as wall.

Classic Revival — Termed also Neoclassicism. A movement which originated in the middle of the eighteenth century, in large measure by writers on art and archaeology. It is distinguished from earlier use of antique art by the effort to imitate exactly the models. *See also* Greek Revival.

Collage — Compositions of fragments of different-coloured and textured materials usually glued (French, coller) to a board or canvas. The shape of the pieces and their manner of composition follows the practices of Cubism. The more extreme examples are also known as *Trash* compositions.

Cubism — The name applied to a revolutionary approach to form in painting, sculpture and architecture, beginning about 1906. In painting and sculpture this approach entailed a description of visible phenomena in terms of their underlying geometrical foundation in many facets. Such a process of careful separation into pieces is often known as *Analytic Cubism*. After 1912 the assembly of fragments into compositions formed the phase of *Synthetic Cubism*. In architecture Cubism can be applied to the simplification of volumes into box-like units, often intricately linked together internally and to the space around the building. Cubism in sculpture lays a stress on both solid and hollow volumes.

Dada — A child's designation of a hobby-horse (in French). A deliberately nonsensical name for objects as removed as possible from what is generally accepted as art. *Dadaism* reached its peak between 1915 and 1922.

Ex-Votos, or Votive Paintings — Paintings which have been dedicated to the saints or Holy Family in fulfilment of a vow to rescue the donor from some dangerous situation. The painting illustrates, usually, the one to whom it is dedicated, the donor, and the special condition that prompted the vow. Though not invariably, the painter as well as his patron were people of simple estate. *Ex-votos* were to be found in Europe, and later in America, from the fifteenth century.

Fauves, Les—(French, Wild Beasts)—The name given in scorn to a small group of French painters who exhibited together in a separate room at the Autumn Salon exhibition, Paris, 1905. The best known were Matisse, Rouault, Derain, Vlaminck. The bright colour and flat simple patterns gained them this name as representatives of a subhuman and violent kind of art.

Futurism — A movement in painting or sculpture which had its beginning in 1909 and died about 1915. Italian in its origin and in the majority of its exponents, it wished to depict human figures and mechanical forms in motion especially by the process of repeating parts of the silhouette. It had roots in the angular splintered shapes of Cubism and in the violent patterns of Expressionism. Rapid movement was taken to be a major characteristic of modern times and of the future, hence the name.

Gothic Revival — A movement taking as its model mediaeval architecture of the thirteenth to the fifteenth centuries. In the eighteenth century historical accuracy was slight, in the post Napoleonic war generation precision became the goal, and the thirteenth century was preferred as representing the peak of mediaeval art.

Greek Revival — A late development within the Classic Revival movement wherein the models of Greek art were followed. The knowledge of Greek art was slight before the nineteenth century. The Greek Revival was particularly influential in the field of architecture.

Impressionism — A name given in scorn in 1874 by adverse critics to the most long lived and productive movement of the nineteenth century. In its most basic form Impressionist painting tried to record the momentary effect of natural phenomena without pose or artificial compositions. Although not invariably, it was most concerned with light as the source of all knowledge of form. Because light is so changing, the observation of light had to be rapid; because it is so complex, light was studied on the spot and the painting completed there. Impressionism also contributed much to new compositional methods derived in large measure from Japanese prints.

International Style — A term used to describe the architecture of the 1920's, the characteristics of which were much the same in all European and American examples. The buildings were box-like in form, used modern materials and techniques, and in style were marked by extreme restraint of ornament and the composition of interior spaces in overlapping volumes of adjacent areas, by the use of screens and transparent separations.

Italian Villa — Term used to describe houses built in a style that borrowed most of its decorative details from Italian Renaissance architecture. The composition of the building masses was asymmetrical, the silhouette broken by towers. As the name villa implies the house was based on the less formal country house architecture of Italy which was well known to travellers and to those familiar with seventeenth century paintings and drawings by Claude Lorrain. The style had its vogue in England from c.1800, in America from 1835.

Lithograph — A method of printing invented at the beginning of the nineteenth century. A greasy crayon is used to draw the design on a porous stone surface that when wet repels a greasy ink which will adhere, however, to the greasy design. Paper pressed against the stone takes the ink from the design. It is the only common method of direct transfer. An artist can reproduce his drawing without a slow process of engraving. Immediate impressions can be quickly reproduced. The process is especially valuable for mass reproduction because there is virtually no wear during printing. It was much used by artists for posters and for caricatures in newspaper illustration.

Moorish Revival — Architecture of the first half of the nineteenth century which showed certain Islamic characteristics, notably horseshoe arches, onion-shaped domes, and large areas of repeated ornamental patterns.

Naïve — Used as an adjective to describe painters in whom are combined untrained talents and a desire to imitate familiar themes of painting. Sometimes known as *Sunday painters*, by reason of their spare time activities as painters; and as *Primitives*, although they are not the first or prime stage of an historical development. Most naïve painters tend to render space in two dimensions, and stress emphatic pattern devices like symmetry and obvious rhythmic repetitions. Details are rendered precisely, outstanding characteristics of things are stressed, movement and change are rarely suggested.

Pointillism — The technique of uniform application of small areas of paint to produce optical colour mixing, and a conspicuous texture of surface on the canvas. Used by the Post Impressionists.

Post Impressionism — A term used to describe the change which immediately followed Impressionism, in the 1880's and 1890's. Called also *Neo-Impressionism*. Optical colour mixing invented by the Impressionist painters was converted into a system with rules of procedure that made possible large pictures in elaborate compositions because the painter was freed from the need to record at the moment what he saw. The method was first used by G. Seurat in 1884. *See Pointillism*.

Primitive—see Naïve.

Romanesque Revival — Architecture of the second and third quarter of the nineteenth century which followed twelfth century Romanesque forms for decorative detail. Heavy short towers and domes, large round arches, heavy random stone facings of walls, and ornamental mouldings and capitals derived from twelfth century models are characteristics. This revival was known also as *Norman* in English-speaking countries.

Romantic Painting — The movement in opposition to Neo-Classicism which sought to arouse strong expressions of feeling by the representations of violent or strange actions painted in colours which in themselves excited the senses strongly.

Random — The arrangement of stone in various heights and lengths in a wall. In practice the range is restricted so that no stone is distractingly large or small or inordinately thin. In modern practice the face is rarely smooth but somewhat roughly finished and generally squared. Such a wall is rich in variety of surface texture and in light and shadow effects. Furthermore it has certain *Primitive* qualities which are admired today.

Surrealism — An artistic movement having as its intention the direction of the artist by his subconscious mind. Although it had its official beginning only in 1922, Surrealism merely gave a clear definition of much modern paintings since about 1906/7 wherever the artist had painted how he felt, not what he saw. Surrealism which used many of the terms and notions of modern psychology grew in two directions, as pure fantasy or as the representation of elaborate dream imagery. It is as much a literary movement as artistic. Although it has produced little of lasting value, the widespread interest among artists and public in psychoanalysis has guaranteed it a considerable influence on post-World War II movements like Action Painting, etc.

Synthetic Cubism — see Cubism.

Topographical Painting — The kind of painting which aims to illustrate specific natural features, as much for information as to please the eye. Most topographical art had as its goal some printing process by which the illustrations might be generally circulated, in books or single sheets. It was superseded by the camera.

Trash Compositions — see Collage.

Index

Illustrations

CHAPTER I

ARCHITECTURE: THE NINETEENTH CENTURY

CHAPTER II

PAINTING: THE NINETEENTH CENTURY

CHAPTER III

PAINTING: THE 20TH CENTURY

CHAPTER IV

MODERN MOVEMENTS IN SCULPTURE

CHAPTER V

MODERN MOVEMENTS IN ARCHITECTURE

CHAPTER VI

AMERICAN ART

CHAPTER VII

CANADIAN ART

CHAPTER VIII

THE ARTS OF PRIMITIVE PEOPLES

CHAPTER IX

ART OF EASTERN ASIA

Colour Plates